## CUTE AND EASY
# Crocheted
# Baby Clothes

# CUTE AND EASY
# Crocheted
# Baby Clothes

## 35 ADORABLE PROJECTS FOR 0–3 YEAR OLDS

## Nicki Trench

CICO BOOKS
LONDON  NEW YORK

Published in 2012 by CICO Books
an imprint of Ryland Peters & Small Ltd
519 Broadway, 5th Floor
New York NY 10012

www.cicobooks.com

10 9 8 7 6 5 4 3 2 1

A CIP catalogue record for this book is
available from the Library of Congress.

ISBN: 978 1 908170 48 4

Printed in China

Editor: Marie Clayton
Designer: Elizabeth Healey
Photographer: Penny Wincer
Stylist: Luis Peral-Aranda
Techniques illustrators: Kate Simunek
and Stephen Dew

For digital editions, visit
www.cicobooks.com/apps.php

# Contents

# Introduction

**THERE IS AN ABUNDANCE** of crochet in stores at the moment, so why not make your baby trendy, too? In this book we have brought you a range of baby clothes and accessories designed to delight. It doesn't matter if you're experienced or a beginner; there are projects to suit all and we've marked levels on each pattern so you can see which one suits your ability best: Beginner, Improver, or Enthusiast.

Many of the designs have been influenced by vintage patterns and, in particular, those belonging to my mother that she made when I was a child. If you've been put off by old-fashioned baby bonnets made in yarn that would either make your baby's hair stand on end or come out in a rash, think again. Our contemporary versions will have you eagerly heading to your yarn store or internet supplier.

We've chosen really pretty colors to show off the projects and embellished them with tiny flowers, embroidery, or ribbons. You don't have to stick with the traditional blue for boy and pink for girl theme; feel free to experiment with the delicious colors available.

I've mostly used the brand "Rooster Yarns" for the projects, simply because it's great to crochet with. It is made from a mix of baby alpaca and merino wool and is supersoft against the baby's skin. It's also 100 percent natural, allowing the yarn to "breathe" in the summer and still keep the baby warm in winter. If you're substituting something else, make sure you use a really soft yarn for delicate baby skins and where possible use wool rather than acrylic.

Many people are thrown into a panic by crochet patterns. This is a big part of learning to crochet. I still have a pencil next to me when I'm crocheting and mark off every row, even every stitch if it's a new technique I'm just learning. Follow the pattern row by row exactly and you won't go wrong. We have a Techniques section in the book too, with clear illustrations that will help you out of a tight spot if you need to learn something new, or just need a reminder.

Most of the garments in the book come in different sizes so the patterns can have lots of numbers; it's essential to circle the size you're following before you start. It's always best to read a pattern through before beginning—it makes good bedtime reading instead of that dull romantic novel!

Making things for a baby is completely satisfying, whether you're crocheting for your own baby as you sit anticipating its birth, or making a gift for family or friends. Most of the projects in this book are small and quick, or try one of the blankets or shawls—they could take the whole nine months!

# Techniques

In this section, we explain how to master the simple crochet techniques that you need to make the projects in this book.

### Making a slip knot
The simplest way is to make a circle with the yarn, so that the loop is facing downward.

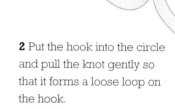

**1** In one hand hold the circle at the top, where the yarn crosses, and let the tail drop down so that it falls in the center of the loop. With your free hand or the tip of a crochet hook, pull the tail through the loop and pull the knot, so that it tightens loosely.

**2** Put the hook into the circle and pull the knot gently so that it forms a loose loop on the hook.

### Holding the hook
Pick up your hook as though you were picking up a pen or pencil. Keeping the hook held loosely between your fingers and thumb, turn your hand so that the palm is facing up and the hook is balanced in your hand and resting in the space between your index finger and your thumb.

## Holding yarn

Pick up the yarn with your little finger in the opposite hand to your hook, with your palm facing upward. Turn your hand to face downward, with the yarn on top of your index finger and under the other two fingers and wrapped right around the little finger. Keeping your index finger only at a slight curve, hold your work just under the slip knot with the other hand.

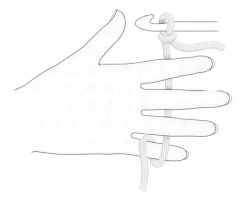

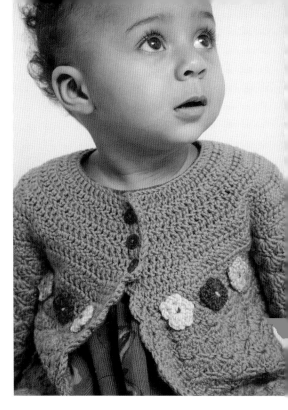

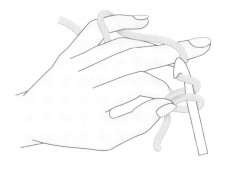

## Yarn over

To create a stitch, you'll need to catch the yarn with the hook and pull it through the loop. Holding your yarn and hook correctly, catch the yarn from behind with the hook pointed upward. As you gently pull the yarn through the loop on the hook, turn the hook so that it faces downward and slide the yarn through the loop. The loop on the hook should be kept loose enough so that the hook slides through easily.

## Chain

**1** Using the hook, wrap the yarn over the hook and pull it through the loop on the hook, creating a new loop on the hook. Continue in this way to create a chain of the required length.

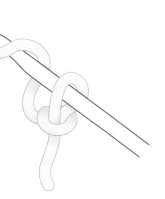

**2** Keep moving your middle finger and thumb close to the hook, to hold the work in place with the opposite hand that you hold your hook with.

## Chain ring/circle

If you are crocheting a round shape, one way of starting off is by crocheting a number of chains following the instructions in your pattern, and then joining them into a circle.

**1** To join the chain into a circle, insert the crochet hook into the first chain that you made (not into the slip knot), yarn over hook, then pull the yarn through the chain and through the loop on your hook at the same time, thereby creating a slip stitch and forming a circle.

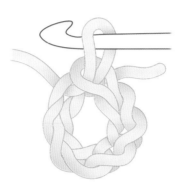

**2** You will now have a circle ready according to your pattern.

*Some of the circles in this book have been made by creating a spiral, whereby you make two chains and insert your hook into the second chain from the hook (the first chain you made). Following the instructions in the pattern will then ensure the spiral has the correct amount of stitches. It's essential to use a stitch marker when using this method, so that you know where to start and finish your round.*

## Marking rounds

Place a stitch marker at the beginning of each round; a piece of yarn in a contrasting color is useful for this. Loop the stitch marker into the first stitch; when you have made a round and reached the point where the stitch marker is, work this stitch, take out the stitch marker from the previous round and put it back into the first stitch of the new round.

## Joining new yarn

If using single crochet, insert the hook as normal into the stitch, using the original yarn, and pull a loop through. Drop the old yarn and pick up the new yarn. Wrap the new yarn over the hook and pull it through the two loops on the hook.

## Slip stitch

A slip stitch doesn't create any height and is often used as the last stitch to create a smooth and even round or row.

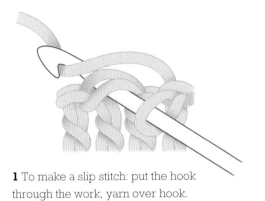

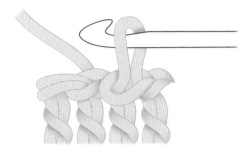

**1** To make a slip stitch: put the hook through the work, yarn over hook.

**2** Pull the yarn through both the work and through the loop on the hook at the same time.

## Single crochet

**1** Insert the hook into your work, yarn over hook and pull the yarn through the work. You will then have two loops on the hook.

**2** Yarn over hook again and pull through the two loops on the hook. You will then have one loop on the hook.

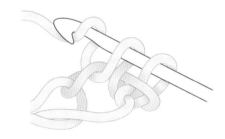

## Half double

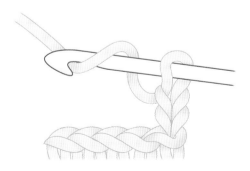

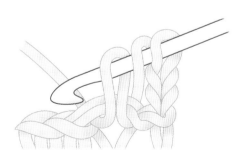

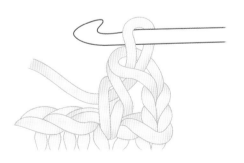

**1** Before inserting the hook into the work, wrap the yarn over the hook and put the hook through the work with the yarn wrapped around.

**2** Yarn over hook again and pull through the first loop on the hook (you now have three loops on the hook).

**3** Yarn over hook and pull the yarn through all three loops. You'll be left with one loop on the hook.

## Double crochet

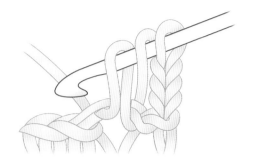  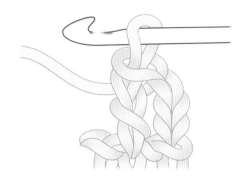

**1** Before inserting the hook into the work, wrap the yarn over the hook and put the hook through the work with the yarn wrapped around.

**2** Yarn over hook again and pull through the first loop on the hook (you now have three loops on the hook). Yarn over hook again, pull the yarn through two loops (you now have two loops on the hook).

**3** Pull the yarn through two loops again. You will be left with one loop on the hook.

## Treble

Yarn over hook twice, insert hook into the stitch, yarn over hook, pull a loop through (four loops on hook), yarn over hook, pull the yarn through two stitches (three loops on hook), yarn over hook, pull a loop through the next two stitches (two loops on hook), yarn over hook, pull a loop through the last two stitches.

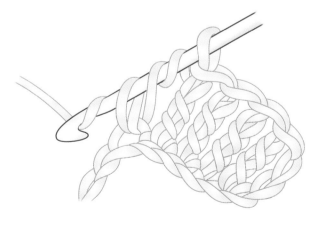

## Double treble

Yarn over hook three times, insert hook into the stitch, yarn over hook, pull a loop through (five loops on hook), yarn over hook, pull the yarn through two stitches (four loops on hook), yarn over hook, pull a loop through the next two stitches (three loops on hook), yarn over hook, pull a loop through the next two stitches (two loops on hook), yarn over hook, pull a loop through the last two stitches.

## Triple treble

For trtr, begin by wrapping the yarn over the hook four times and then proceed in the same way as for Double Treble until you are left with one loop on the hook.

## Loop stitch

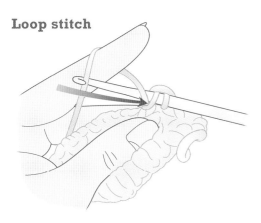

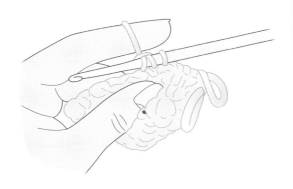

**1** With the yarn over the left index finger, insert the hook into the next stitch and draw two strands through the stitch (take the first strand from under the index finger and at the same time take the second strand from over the index finger).

**2** Pull the yarn to tighten the loop, forming a 1in. (2.5cm) loop on the index finger. Remove finger from the loop, put the loop to the back of the work, yarn over hook and pull through three loops on the hook (1 loop stitch made on right side of work).

## Making rows

A turning chain is needed at the end of a row to create the height for the stitch, as follows:

Single crochet = 1 chain
Half double crochet = 2 chain
Double crochet = 3 chain
Treble crochet = 4 chain
Double treble crochet = 5 chain
Triple treble crochet = 6 chain

## Intarsia

Use small balls of yarn; one each side of the motif, and one or more for the motif. Use the background color to one stitch before the motif; change color by bringing in the motif color on the last pull through of the stitch. Crochet the motif stitch(es) as per the chart; one stitch before the end of the motif change to the background color in the same way. Keep color changes to the WS of the work.

## Chain space

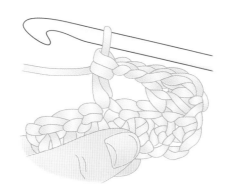

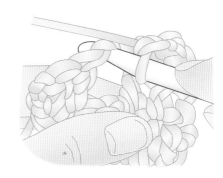

**1** A chain space (ch sp) is the space that has been made under a chain in the previous round or row, and falls in between other stitches.

**2** Stitches into a chain space are made directly into the hole created under the chain and not into the chain stitches themselves.

### Decreasing

You can decease by either missing the next stitch and continuing to crochet, or by crocheting two or more stitches together. The basic technique is the same no matter which stitch you are using; the illustration shows working three doubles (dc3tog) in progress:

Work a double crochet into each of the next three stitches as normal, but leave the last loop of each stitch on the hook (four loops on the hook). Yarn over hook and pull the yarn through all the stitches on the hook to join them together. You will finish with one loop on the hook.

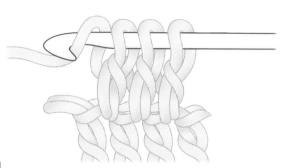

### Increasing

Make two or three stitches into one stitch from the previous row. The illustration shows a two-stitch increase being made.

### Single crochet two stitches together

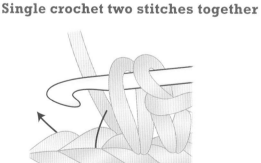

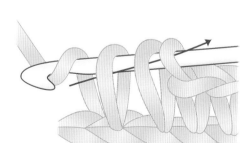

**1** Insert hook into next stitch, draw a loop through, insert hook into next stitch.

**2** Draw a loop through, yarn over hook and pull through all three stitches.

## Half double two stitches together

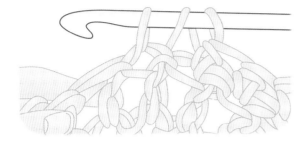

**1** Yarn over hook, insert hook into next stitch, yarn over hook, draw yarn through (three loops on hook).

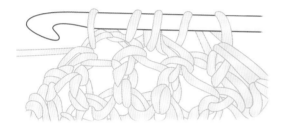

**2** Yarn over hook, insert hook into next stitch, yarn over hook, draw yarn through.

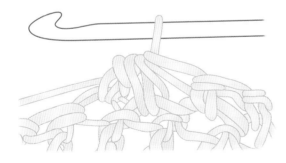

**3** Draw yarn through all five loops on hook.

### Fastening off

Cut the yarn leaving a tail of approx. 4in (10cm). Pull the tail all the way through the loop.

### How to single crochet squares together

Place two squares wrong sides together, lining them up so that the stitches on each square match. Put the hook through the top loops of the first square and also through the corresponding top loops of the second square. Join in the yarn, make 1 chain, insert the hook into the top stitches of both squares, and make a single crochet seam across the top of the squares.

# CHAPTER ONE

# Sweaters and Cardigans

# Springtime Sweater

A warm and cozy sweater, the squares, based on the traditional "granny square," are easy for beginners; it's in the "Improver" category only because of the picot and neck shaping.

## Materials

**50% baby alpaca/50% merino mix light worsted (DK) yarn, such as Rooster Almerino DK**

→ 3 x 1¾oz (50g) balls—approx. 372yds (337.5m)—of off-white (MC)
→ 1 x 1¾oz (50g) ball—approx. 124yds (112.5m)—each of pale pink (A), rust (B), pale blue (C), yellow (D), green (E), and purple
→ F/5 (4mm) crochet hook

## Abbreviations

**ch** chain; **ch sp** chain space; **dc** double crochet; **hdc** half double crochet; **MC** main color; **rep** repeat; **RS** right side; **sc** single crochet; **sp** space; **ss** slip stitch; **st(s)** stitch(es); **WS** wrong side; **yo** yarn over hook

## Special abbreviations

**dc2tog** (double crochet 2 together decrease) *yo, insert hook in next st, yo, pull yarn through, yo, pull yarn through 2 loops on hook (2 loops on hook). Without finishing st, rep from * in next st (3 loops on hook), yo, pull yarn through all 3 loops on hook

**hdc2tog** (half double crochet 2 together decrease) *yo, insert hook in next st, yo, pull yarn through (3 loops on hook). Without finishing st, rep from * in next st (5 loops on hook), yo, pull yarn through all 5 loops on hook

## Size

**To fit age**: 12–24 months

## Finished size

**Chest**: 23in. (57.5cm)
**Length**: 13in. (32.5cm)
**Sleeve Seam**: 7½in. (19cm)

## Gauge

1 square measures approx. 2½in. (6cm) using a F/5 (4mm) hook. Sleeves: 20 sts x 14 rows over a 4in. (10cm) square working half double crochet using a F/5 (4mm) hook.

## Square (make 30)

Use different color combinations on each
square; always use MC for Round 2.

Using first color, make a loop, make 4ch, join
with ss in first ch to form a ring.

**Round 1**: 3ch, 2dc in ring, 2ch, 3dc in ring,
2ch, *3dc in ring, 2ch; rep from * once more,
ss in top of first 3ch.

   Fasten off.

   Put hook in any ch sp, join in MC.

**Round 2**: 3ch, 2dc, 3ch, 3dc in same ch sp
(first corner), 2ch, *3dc, 3ch, 3dc in next ch sp,
2ch; rep from * twice more, ss in top of first 3ch.

   Fasten off.

   Put hook in top of fasten off st, join in third
color, make 1ch.

**Round 3**: 1sc in top of next 2 sts, 3sc in next
ch sp, 1sc in top of next 3 sts, 2sc in next ch
sp, *1sc in top of next 3 sts, 3sc in next ch sp,
1sc in top of next 3 sts, 2sc in next ch sp; rep
from * twice more, ss in top of first ch.

   Fasten off.

   Sew in ends neatly and securely after
making each square.

## Back (16 squares)

Using sc seams, join strips of four squares
across by four squares down to make a 16-
square panel.

## Front (14 squares)

Using sc seams, join together strips of four
squares across by three squares down.

   To create hole for neck join one square on
each outside strip (left and right of front).

## Shoulders

Using MC and with RS facing, join yarn in top
right corner of front piece and work in dc:

**Row 1**: 1ch, 1dc in each st across square.

Fasten off.

**Row 2**: Using A, join yarn at beginning (not end) of previous row in top of first 3-ch, 3ch, 1dc in each st across.

Fasten off.

**Row 3**: Using B, join yarn at beginning (not end) of previous row in top of first 3-ch, 3ch, 1dc in each st across.

Fasten off.

Rep on other shoulder, joining yarn and starting at top outside edge.

**Joining shoulders:**
Using a yarn needle and suitable yarn color, join shoulder seams.

## Neck
With RS facing, join MC in back of neck at right side of jumper in corner st of shoulder and sc joining seam of square and work in hdc:

**Row 1**: 2ch, 1hdc in each st across back (30 sts), 2hdc in each color (row end from shoulders, 6 sts), 1hdc in each st down left front edge (11 sts), 1hdc in corner seam st, 1hdc in next and each st across center front (27 sts), 1hdc in corner seam st, 1hdc in next and each st up right front (12 sts), 2hdc in each color (row end from shoulders), 1hdc in corner seam, (7 sts), join with ss in first 2-ch. (93 sts)

Join in B.

**Row 2**: 2ch, [1hdc in each of next 8 sts, hdc2tog] three times, 1hdc in each of next 2 sts, hdc2tog, 1hdc in each of next 9 sts, hdc2tog, [1hdc in each of next 6 sts, hdc2tog] four times, 1hdc in each of next 9 sts, hdc2tog, 1hdc in next 2 sts, hdc2tog, 1hdc in shoulder seam, join with ss in top of first 2-ch. (83 sts)

Join in C.

**Row 3**: 2ch, [1hdc in each of next 7 sts, hdc2tog] three times, 1hdc in next st, hdc2tog, 1hdc in each of next 8 sts, [dc2tog] four times, 1hdc in each of next 6 sts, dc2tog, 1hdc in each of next 6 sts, [dc2tog] four times, 1hdc in each

of next 7 sts, hdc2tog, 1hdc in each of next 2 sts, hdc2tog, 1hdc in next next st, join with ss in top of first 2-ch. (68 sts)

Join in A.

**Row 4**: 2ch, 1hdc in each of next 5 sts, hdc2tog, 1hdc in each of next 7 sts, hdc2tog, 1hdc in each of next 7 sts, hdc2tog, 1hdc in each of next 7 sts, [dc2tog] three times, 1hdc in each of next 5 sts, hdc2tog, 1hdc in each of next 6 sts, [dc2tog] three times, 1hdc in each of next 7 sts, hdc2tog, 1hdc in each of next 3 sts, ss in top of first 2-ch.

Join in MC.

**Row 5 (picot)**: *3ch, ss in same st, 3ch, ss in next st; rep from * to end.
Fasten off.

## Sides
### Left side (back):
With RS facing, join MC at side edge of back piece in second square down from shoulder and in center stitch of square, 1ch, 1sc in each st to bottom edge.

Join in D.

**Next row**: 1sc in each st to end.
Fasten off.

### Left side (front):
With RS facing, join MC in bottom corner st, 1ch, 1sc in each st to center st of second square from shoulder.

Join in E.

**Next row**: 1sc in each st to end.
Fasten off.

### Right side (back):
With RS facing, join MC at side edge in bottom corner st, 1ch, 1sc in each st to center st of second square from shoulder.

Join in D.

**Next row**: 1sc in each st to end.
Fasten off.

### Right side (front):
With RS facing, join in E at side edge of front

piece, in second square down from shoulder and in center st of square, 1ch, 1sc in each st to bottom edge.

Join in MC.

**Next row**: 1sc in each st to end.
Fasten off.

## Bottom
### Front:
With WS facing, join in D in left corner of bottom edge, 2ch, 1hdc in each row end of side panel, 1hdc in each st along bottom edge (of squares), 1hdc in each row end of second side panel. Break yarn.

Join in C.

**Next row**: 2ch, 1hdc in each st to end. Break yarn.

Join in B.

**Next row**: 2ch, 1hdc in each st to end. Break yarn.

Join in MC.

**Next row (picot)**: *3ch, 1ss in same st, 1ss in next st; rep from * to end.

Fasten off.

Rep for back.

With WS facing join side panel seams.

## Sleeves
With RS facing, join MC in underarm st at front.

**Row 1**: 2ch, using hdc, make 48 sts evenly around sleeve edge (hdc2tog in last sts if necessary to achieve 48 sts), turn.

**Row 2**: 2ch, 1hdc in each st to end, ss in top of first 2-ch, turn.

**Row 3**: 2ch, 1hdc in each st to end, ss in top of first 2-ch, turn.

**Row 4**: 2ch, 1hdc in next st, hdc2tog, 1hdc in each st to last 3 sts, hdc2tog, 1hdc in last st, turn. (46 sts)

**Row 5**: Rep Row 4. (44 sts)

**Row 6**: Rep Row 4. (42 sts)

**Row 7**: Rep Row 4. (40 sts)

**Row 8**: 2ch, 1hdc in each st to end, ss in top of first 2-ch, turn.

**Row 9**: Rep Row 8.

**Row 10**: Rep Row 4. (38 sts)

**Row 11**: Rep Row 8.

**Row 12**: Rep Row 2.

**Row 13**: Rep Row 4. (36 sts)

**Rows 14–15**: Rep Row 2.

**Row 16**: Rep Row 4. (34 sts)

**Rows 17–18**: Rep Row 2.

**Row 19**: Rep Row 4. (32 sts)

**Rows 20–21**: Rep Row 2.

**Row 22**: Rep Row 4. (30 sts) Break yarn.

**Sleeve cuffs:**

Join in D.

**Row 1**: 1ch, 1sc in first st, *sc2tog, 1sc in each of next 2 sts; rep from * to end, ss in first 1-ch. Break yarn.

Join in C.

**Row 2**: 1ch, 1sc in each st to end. Break yarn.

Join in B.

**Row 3**: Rep Row 2. Break yarn.

Join in A.

**Row 4**: Rep Row 2. Break yarn.

Join in MC.

**Row 5**: Ss in next st, *3ch, ss in same st, ss in next st; rep from * to end.

Fasten off.

**Finishing**

With WS facing, join sleeve seams. Sew in ends.

# Wrapover Cardigan

A very pretty cardigan which is perfect
for growing babies as it wraps over
rounded tummies.

## Materials

**50% baby alpaca/50% merino mix light worsted (DK) yarn, such as
Rooster Almerino DK**

➔ 2:3:3:4 x 1¾oz (50g) balls—approx. 248:372:372:496yds
(225:337.5:337.5:450m)—of off-white (A)

**50% baby alpaca/50% merino light worsted (DK) yarn, such as
Rooster Almerino Baby**

➔ 1 x 1¾oz (50g) ball—approx. 136½yds (125m)—of pink (B)

➔ D/3 (3mm) crochet hook

## Abbreviations

**ch** chain; **dc** double crochet; **rep** repeat; **RS** right side; **sc** single crochet;
**sc2tog** (single crochet 2 together decrease) insert hook in next st, yo, pull
yarn through (2 loops on hook). Without finishing st, insert hook in next st, yo,
pull yarn through (3 loops on hook), yo, pull yarn through all 3 loops on hook;
**ss** slip stitch; **st(s)** stitch(es); **yo** yarn over hook

## Special abbreviations

**dc2tog** (double crochet 2 together decrease) *yo, insert hook in next st, yo,
pull yarn through, yo, pull yarn through 2 loops on hook (2 loops on hook).
Without finishing st, rep from * in next st (3 loops on hook), yo, pull yarn
through all 3 loops on hook

**dc3tog** (double crochet 3 together decrease) *yo, insert hook in next st, yo,
pull yarn through, yo, pull yarn through 2 loops on hook (2 loops on hook).
Without finishing st, rep from * in each of next 2 sts (4 loops on hook), yo, pull
yarn through all 4 loops on hook

## Size

**To fit age**: 0–3:3–6:6–12:12–18 months

## Finished size

| Chest | (in.): | 17¼ | 19¼ | 21½ | 23½ |
|---|---|---|---|---|---|
| | (cm): | 44 | 49 | 54 | 59 |
| Length | (in.): | 7½ | 8¼ | 10½ | 11½ |
| | (cm): | 19 | 20.5 | 26.5 | 29 |
| Sleeve seam | (in.): | 5 | 6¼ | 7¾ | 9½ |
| | (cm): | 12.5 | 15.5 | 19.5 | 24 |

## Gauge

18 sts x 10 rows over a 4in. (10cm) square working double crochet using
a D/3 (3mm) hook.

## Body

Using A, make 123:**140**:150:**167**ch.

**Row 1**: 1sc in second ch from hook, 1sc in each ch to end.

**Rows 2–4**: 3ch, 1dc in each st to end. (122:**139**:149:**166** sts)

**Shape front slopes:**

Sc2tog twice at each end of next 4:**7**:8:**10** rows. (106:**111**:117:**126** sts)

Body should now measure approx. 3¼:**4**:5:5½in. (8:**10**:12.5:**14**cm).

**Divide for armholes, first front:**

**Row 1**: Dc3tog at front edge, 1dc in each of next 19:**21**:23:**26** sts, dc3tog at armhole edge, turn. (21:**23**:25:**28** sts)

**Row 2**: Dc2tog twice at armhole edge, 1dc in each st to last 4 sts, dc2tog twice at front edge. (17:**19**:21:**24** sts)

**Row 3**: Dc2tog twice at front edge, 1dc in each st to last 4 sts, dc2tog twice at armhole edge. (13:**15**:17:**20** sts)

**Row 4**: Dc2tog twice at front edge, 1dc in each st to end. (11:**13**:15:**18** sts)

**Row 5**: 1dc in each st to end. (11:**13**:15:**18** sts)

**Row 6**: 1dc in each st to last 4 sts, dc2tog twice. (9:**11**:13:**16** sts)

**Rows 7–9**: 1dc in each st. (9:**11**:13:**16** sts)

**Row 10**: 1dc in each st to last 2 sts, dc2tog. (8:**10**:12:**15** sts)

Size 0–3 months, fasten off.

**Row 11**: Dc2tog, 1dc in each st to end. (8:**9**:11:**14** sts)

**Rows 12–13**: 1dc in each st to end. (8:**9**:11:**14** sts)

Size 3–6 months, fasten off.

**Row 14**: 1dc in each st to last 2 sts, dc2tog. (8:**9**:10:**12** sts)

Size 6–12 months, fasten off.

**Row 15**: Dc2tog, 1dc in each st to end. (8:**9**:10:**11** sts)

Size **12–18** months, fasten off.

**Shape back:**

Return to last complete row worked of body before arm shaping.

**Row 1**: Skip 3 sts, join yarn to next st, dc3tog, 1dc in each of next 42:**45**:47:**50** sts, dc3tog, turn. (44:**47**:49:**52** sts)

**Row 2**: Dc2tog twice at each end of row. (40:**43**:45:**48** sts)

**Row 3**: Dc2tog twice at each end of row. (36:**39**:41:**44** sts)

**Rows 4–10**: 1dc in each st to end. (36:**39**:41:**44** sts)

**Shape back, neck, and shoulder:**

1dc in each of next 7:**8**:9:**10** sts, dc3tog. (8:**9**:10:**11** sts)

Fasten off.

Return to last complete row worked of body before shaping back neck.

Skip next 16:**17**:17:**18** sts, join yarn to next st.

Dc3tog, 1dc in each st to end.

Fasten off.

**Second front:**

Return to last complete row worked of body before arm shaping.

**Row 1**: Skip 3 sts, dc3tog, 1dc in each of next 19:**21**:23:**26** sts, dc3tog. (21:**23**:25:**28** sts)

**Row 2**: 3ch, dc2tog twice, 1dc in each st to last 4 sts, dc2tog twice. (17:**19**:21:**24** sts)

**Row 3**: Dc2tog twice at armhole edge, 1dc in each st to last 4 sts, dc2tog twice. (13:**15**:17:**20** sts)

**Row 4**: Dc2tog twice at front edge. (11:**13**:15:**18** sts)

**Row 5**: 3ch, 1dc in each st to end. (11:**13**:15:**18** sts)

**Row 6**: Dc2tog twice, 1dc in each st to end. (9:**11**:13:**16** sts)

**Rows 7–9**: 1dc in each st. (9:**11**:13:**16** sts)

**Row 10**: Dc2tog, 1dc in each st to end. (8:**10**:12:**15** sts)

Size 0–3 months, fasten off.

**Row 11**: 1dc in each st to last 3 sts, dc2tog. (8:**9**:11:**14** sts)

**Rows 12–13**: 1dc in each st. (8:**9**:11:**14** sts)

Size 3–6 months, fasten off.

**Rows 14**: Dc2tog, 1dc in each st to end. (8:**9**:10:**12** sts)

Size 6–12 months, fasten off.

**Row 15**: 1dc in each st to last 2 sts, dc2tog. (8:**9**:10:**11** sts)

Size **12–18** months, fasten off.

## Sleeves (make 2)

Using A, make 27:**33**:37:**37**ch.

**Row 1**: 1ch, 1sc in each ch to end. (26:**32**:36:**36** sts)

**Row 2**: 1ch, 1sc in each st to end. (26:**32**:36:**36** sts)

**Row 3**: 3ch, 1dc in each st to end.

**Row 4**: 3ch, 2dc in next st, 1dc in each st to last 2 sts, 2dc in next st, 1dc in top of 3-ch from previous row. (29:**35**:39:**39** sts)

**Rows 5–6**: 3ch, 1dc in each st to last st, 1dc in top of 3-ch from previous row. (30:**36**:40:**40** sts)

**Row 7**: 3ch, 1dc in next st, 2dc in next st, 1dc in each st to last 2 sts, 2dc in next st, 1dc in next st, 1dc in top of 3-ch from previous row. (33:**39**:43:**43** sts)

**Row 8**: 3ch, 1dc in each st to end, 1dc in top of 3-ch from previous row. (34:**40**:44:**44** sts)

**Row 9**: 3ch, 1dc in each st to end, 1dc in top of 3-ch from previous row. (35:**41**:45:**45** sts)

**Size 0–3 months only:**

**Row 10**: Rep Row 8. (36 sts)

Work straight in dc until sleeve measures 5in. (12.5cm).

**All other sizes:**

Row 10: Rep Row 7. (44:48:48 sts)
Row 11: Rep Row 8. (45:49:49 sts)
Row 12: Rep Row 8. (46:50:50 sts)
Row 13: Rep Row 8. (47:51:51 sts)

Rep Row 7 [0:0:1] times more. (47:51:54 sts)
Work straight in dc until sleeve measures
5:6¼:7¾:9½in. (12.5:15.5:19.5:24cm).

**All sizes shape top:**

Next row: Ss across first 2:3:3:4 sts, dc2tog,
1dc in each st to last 4:5:5:6 sts, dc2tog, turn.
(30:39:43:44 sts)

Next row: [Dc2tog] twice, 1dc in each st to
last 4 sts, [dc2tog] twice. (26:35:39:40 sts)

Rep the last row 3:4:5:5 more times.
(14:19:19:20 sts)

Fasten off.

## Finishing

Pin and oversew shoulder seams together.
With right sides together, oversew sleeves
from underarm to wrist.

Fit each sleeve inside main piece with
wrong sides on the inside. Match center top of
sleeve to match to shoulder seam and sleeve
seam to match skipped 3 sts of main body.

Pin and oversew.

## Edging

**Fronts, back, and bottom:**

Using A, join yarn bottom right-hand front
edge with RS facing.

Make 1sc evenly around right side, across
back neck, down left side to bottom corner and
along bottom edge, join with a ss in first sc.

Fasten off.

**Picot edging:**

Using B, join yarn in first sc at base of front
right-hand edge with RS facing.

*3ch, ss in same st, skip 1 st, ss in next st;
rep from * around cardigan edging. Ss in

base of first picot to finish.

Fasten off.

**Sleeve edging:**

Using B, join yarn at the seam, make a Picot
edging around as main body.

## Ties

Using B, join yarn at Row 3 of right front edge.
Make 102:120:134:148ch, 1sc in next ch from

hook and each ch back to front edge, join
with ss. Fasten off leaving a long tail. Sew in
end securely.

Rep Tie instructions on other front edge.

## Finishing

Sew in ends.

Tie ties to fit by slotting one tie through
double crochet holes when fitted on baby.

# Simple Stripy Tank Top

Striped in bright colors,
this works well over pants
or a skirt and keeps your
baby nice and snug.

## Back

Each row is alternated between A and B to form one-row stripes.

Using A, make 46:**50**:54:**58**ch.

**Row 1 (RS):** 1hdc in third ch from hook, 1hdc in each ch to end. (44:**48**:52:**56** sts)

**Next row (WS):** Using B, 2ch, 1hdc in each st.

Cont working straight, striping rows, until work measures 6½:**6½**:8:**9¼**in. (16.5:**16.5**:20:**23**cm) ending with a RS row.

Fasten off.

**Armholes:**

**Row 1 (WS facing):** Skip 5 sts, rejoin yarn in next st, 2ch, 1hdc in each of next 34:**38**:42:**46** sts, leaving last 5 sts unworked. (34:**38**:42:**46** sts) **

Cont working straight until armhole measures 4½:**4½**:5¼:**5¼**in. (11.5:**11.5**:13:**13**cm)

**Shoulders:**

**Next row:** 2ch, work 11:**12**:13:**14** sts.

Fasten off.

Skip next 12:**14**:16:**18** sts, rejoin yarn in next st, 2ch, 1hdc in each of rem 11:**12**:13:**14** sts.

Fasten off.

## Front

Work to ** as for back.

**Next two rows:** 2ch, 1hdc in each st to end. Divide for neck.

**Neck Side 1:**

**Row 1 (WS):** 2ch, 1hdc in each of next 17:**19**:21:**23** sts. (17:**19**:21:**23** sts)

**Row 2:** 2ch, skip 1 st (neck edge), 1hdc in each st to end. (16:**18**:20:**22** sts)

**Row 3:** 2ch, 1hdc in each st to last 2 sts, hdc2tog (neck edge). (15:**17**:19:**21** sts)

Rep Rows 2 and 3 until 11:**12**:13:**14** sts rem.

Work 2ch, 1hdc in each st to end until front measures same length as back.

**Neck Side 2:**

With WS facing, work Side 2 to match Side 1 reversing shaping.

Fasten off.

## Finishing

Join shoulder and side seams.

**Lower edging:**

Using C and with RS facing, join yarn to lower edge at one of the side seams, 1ch, work a round of sc evenly along lower edge, ss in first ch to join round.

Fasten off.

**Neck edging:**

Using C and with RS facing, join yarn at neck edge of one of the shoulder seams.

1ch, make 1sc evenly around neck edge, join with a ss in first ch.

Fasten off.

**Armhole edging:**

Using C and with RS facing, join yarn to top of one of the side seams, 1ch, work a round of sc evenly around armhole, join with a ss in first ch.

Fasten off.

Rep for second armhole.

Sew in ends.

---

## Materials

**50% baby alpaca/50% merino mix light worsted (DK) yarn, such as Rooster Almerino DK**

➜ 1:**1**:2:**2** x 1¾oz (50g) balls—approx. 124:**124**:248:**248**yds (112.5:**112.5**:225:**225**m)—each of off-white (A) and yellow (B)

➜ 1 x 1¾oz (50g) ball—approx. 124yds (112.5m)—of turquoise blue (C)

➜ F/5 (4mm) crochet hook

## Abbreviations

**ch** chain; **cont** continue; **hdc** half double crochet; **rem** remaining; **RS** right side; **sc** single crochet; **ss** slip stitch; **st(s)** stitch(es); **WS** wrong side; **yo** yarn over hook

## Special abbreviation

**hdc2tog** (half double crochet 2 together decrease) *yo, insert hook in next st, yo, pull yarn through (3 loops on hook). Without finishing st, rep from * in next st (5 loops on hook), yo, pull yarn through all 5 loops on hook

## Size

**To fit age:** 3–6:**6–12**:12–18:**24–36** months

## Finished size

| | | | | | |
|---|---|---|---|---|---|
| Chest | (in.): | 21 | 22½ | 25 | 26 |
| | (cm): | 52.5 | **56.5** | 62.5 | **65** |
| Length | (in.): | 11 | **11** | 13 | **14½** |
| | (cm): | 27.5 | **27.5** | 32.5 | **36.5** |
| Armhole to shoulder | (in.): | 4¾ | 4¾ | 5½ | 5½ |
| | (cm): | 12 | **12** | 14 | **14** |

## Gauge

17 sts x 13 rows over a 4in. (10cm) square working half double crochet using a F/5 (4mm) hook.

# Baby Shell Cardigan

A really pretty cardigan for a new baby in the family.
It was inspired by an old vintage-style pattern,
but making it using modern yarns and adding flower
embellishments gives it a modern, yet retro twist.

### Materials

**50% baby alpaca/50% merino light worsted (DK) yarn,
such as Rooster Almerino Baby**

➜ 4:**4** x 1¾oz (50g) balls—approx. 546:**546**yds
(500:**500**m)—of purple (A)

➜ Small amounts of three different shades of pink (B)

➜ D/3 (3mm) and C/2 (2.5mm) crochet hooks

➜ 3 buttons

### Abbreviations

**ch** chain; **cont** continue; **dc** double crochet; **hdc** half double
crochet; **inc** increase; **rep** repeat; **sc** single crochet; **ss** slip
stitch; **st(s)** stitch(es); **WS** wrong side

### Size

**To fit age**: 0–3:**3–6** months

### Finished size

| | | | |
|---|---|---|---|
| **Chest** | **(in.)**: | 19 | 22 |
| | **(cm)**: | 47.5 | 55 |
| **Length** | **(in.)**: | 9 | 11 |
| | **(cm)**: | 22.5 | 27.5 |
| **Sleeve seam** | **(in.)**: | 4 | 4 |
| | **(cm)**: | 10 | 10 |

### Gauge

4 groups of shell pattern x 6 rows of shell pattern over a 4in.
(10cm) square using D/3 (3mm) hook.

## Yoke

Starting at neck edge, and using D/3 (3mm) hook and A, make 60:**71**ch.

**Row 1**: 1dc in third ch from hook, 1dc in each ch. (58:**69** sts)

**Row 2**: 3ch, skip first st, 1dc in each st to end, 1dc in third of 3-ch from previous row.

**Row 3**: 3ch, skip first st, 1dc in each of next 2:**3** sts, *2dc in next st, 1dc in each of next 4:**5** dc; rep from * 9 times more, 2dc in next st, 1dc in each of next 3 sts, 1dc in third of 3-ch from previous row. (69:**80** sts)

**Row 4**: Rep Row 2.

**Row 5**: 3ch, skip first st, 1dc in each of next 3:**4** sts, *inc in next st, 1dc in each of next 5:**6** sts, rep from * 9 times more, inc in next st, 1dc in each of next 3 sts, 1dc in third of 3-ch. (80:**91** sts)

**Row 6**: 3ch, skip first st, 1dc in each st, working inc above inc on previous row, ending with 1dc in third of 3-ch. (91:**102** sts)

Rep Row 6 three times more. (124:**135** sts)

**Row 10**: 3ch, skip first st, 1dc in each of next 4:**5** sts, inc in next st, 1dc in each of next 33:**35** sts, inc in next st, * 1dc in each of next 10:**11** sts, inc in next st; rep from * 3 times more, 1dc in each of next 33:**35** sts, inc in next st, 1dc in each of next 5:**7** sts, 1dc in third of 3-ch. (131:**142** sts)

**Row 11**: 3ch, skip first st, 1dc in each of next 5:**7** sts, inc in next st, 1dc in each of next 12:**14** sts, make 8:**10**ch, skip next 28:**28** sts, 1dc in each of next 6:**7** sts, inc in next st, 1dc in each

of next 23:**25** sts, inc in next st, 1dc in each of next 6:**7** sts, make 8:**10**ch, skip next 25:**27** sts, 1dc in each of next 12:**14** sts, inc in next st, 1dc in each of next 5:**6** sts, 1dc in third of 3-ch. (79:**90** sts)

**Row 12**: 2ch, skip first st, 1sc in each of next 19:**23** sts, 1sc into each of next 8:**10**ch, 1sc into each of next 39:**43** sts, 1sc into each of next 8:**10**ch, 1sc into each of next 19:**22** sts, 1sc in third of 3-ch. (95:**110** sts)

Do not fasten off.

### Skirt 0–3 months:

**Row 1**: 1sc in first sc, *skip 1sc, 5dc in next sc (shell made), skip 1sc, 1sc in next sc, skip 2sc, shell in next sc, skip 2sc, 1sc in next sc;

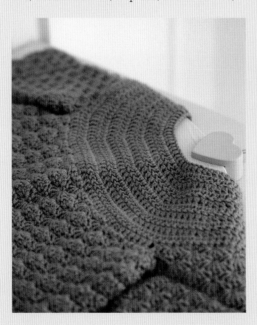

rep from * 8 times more, skip 1sc, 5dc in next sc, skip 1sc, 1sc in next sc.

### Skirt 3–6 months:

**Row 1**: 1sc in first sc, *skip 1sc, 5dc in next sc (shell made), skip 1sc, 1sc in next sc, skip 2sc, shell in next sc, skip 2sc, 1sc in next sc; rep from * 9 times more, skip 1sc, 5dc in next sc, skip 1sc, 1sc in next sc, skip 2sc, shell in next sc, skip 1sc, 1sc in next sc.

### Both sizes:

**Row 2**: 3ch, 2dc in first st (half shell made), *1sc in center dc of next shell, shell in next sc; rep from * ending with 1sc in center dc of last shell, 3dc in last sc.

**Row 3**: 1ch, 1sc in first dc, *shell in next sc, 1sc in center dc of shell; rep from * ending with shell in last sc, 1sc in 3-ch. 3ch.

Rep last 2 rows until skirt measures 5:**7**in. (12.5:**17.5**cm) or length required, ending with a 3rd pattern row.

Fasten off.

### Sleeves

**Round 1**: Attach yarn to 4th:**5th** of 8:**10**ch at underarm, 1sc in each ch, 1sc in each of next 2 row ends, 1sc in next 28:**28** sts, 1sc in each of next 2 row ends, 1sc in each ch, 1ss in first sc. (36:**38** sts)

**Round 2**: *Skip 2 sc, shell in next sc, skip 2 sc, 1sc in next sc; rep from * 6 times more, working last sc in ss.

**Round 3**: 1ss in each of first 2dc, 1sc in next dc, *shell in next sc, 1sc in center dc of next shell; rep from * 6 times more, omitting 1sc at end of last rep, 1ss in first sc.

Rep Round 3 row until sleeve measures 4:**5**in. (10:**12.5**cm).

Fasten off.

## Edging

With RS facing, and using D/3 (3mm) hook and A, attach yarn to neck edge of left front, 1sc in same place as join, *shell in next row end, 1sc in next row end; rep from * 4 times more, shell in next sc row end, 1sc in next sc row end. Cont in this manner down front edges making 1 shell in lower edge corner of each front, 1ss in first sc.

Fasten off.

## Flowers (make 6 in different shades of pink)

Using C/2 (2.5mm) hook and B, make 4ch, join with a ss to form a ring.

*2ch, 1hdc in ring, 2ch, ss in ring; rep from * 4 times more (5 petals).

Fasten off.

Sew in ends, weaving around center to close hole in ring.

Thread yarn needle with contrast color and embroider a French knot in the center.

## Finishing

Sew in ends. Sew 3 buttons to edge of yoke to match position of buttonholes in overlap. Sew flowers at base of yoke.

# Pocket Trim Cardigan

A really simple cardigan to make, with a pretty "granny square" pocket trim.

## Materials

**50% baby alpaca/50% merino mix light worsted (DK) yarn, such as Rooster Almerino DK**

→ 3:**3**:4:**4**:5:**5** x 1¾oz (50g) balls—approx. 372:**372**:496:**496**:620:**620**yds (337.5:**337.5**:450:**450**:562.5:**562.5**m)—of light blue (A)

→ 1 x 1¾oz (50g) ball—approx. 124yds (112.5m)—each of pale yellow (B) and off-white (C)

→ F/5 (4mm) and E/4 (3.5mm) crochet hooks

→ 4:**4**:4:**4**:4:**5** buttons

## Abbreviations

**ch** chain; **dc** double crochet; **hdc** half double crochet; **rep** repeat; **RS** right side; **sc** single crochet; **sc2tog** (single crochet 2 together decrease) insert hook in next st, yo, pull yarn through (2 loops on hook). Without finishing st, insert hook in next st, yo, pull yarn through (3 loops on hook), yo, pull yarn through all 3 loops on hook; **ss** slip stitch; **st(s)** stitch(es); **yo** yarn over hook

## Special abbreviations

**dc2tog** (double crochet 2 together decrease) yo, insert hook in next st, yo, pull yarn through, yo, pull yarn through 2 loops on hook (2 loops), yo, insert hook in next st, yo, pull yarn through, yo, pull yarn through 2 loops on hook (3 loops), yo, pull yarn through all 3 loops on hook

**dc3tog** (double crochet 3 together decrease) yo, insert hook in next st, yo, pull yarn through, yo, pull yarn through 2 loops on hook (2 loops), yo, insert hook in next st, yo, pull yarn through, yo, pull yarn through 2 loops on hook (3 loops), yo, insert hook in next st, yo, pull yarn through, yo, pull yarn through 2 loops on hook (4 loops), yo, pull yarn through all 4 loops on hook

## Size

**To fit age:** 0–3:**3–6**:6–12:**12–18**:18–24:**24–36** months

## Finished size

| Chest | (in.) | 19 | 20½ | 25 | 26 | 27 | 28 |
|---|---|---|---|---|---|---|---|
| | (cm) | 47.5 | **51.5** | 62.5 | **65** | 67.5 | 70 |
| Length | (in.) | 10½ | 10½ | 11½ | 13 | 14 | 15 |
| | (cm) | 26.5 | **26.5** | 29 | **32.5** | 35 | 37.5 |
| Sleeve seam | (in.) | 4 | 4 | 4½ | 5 | 5½ | 5¾ |
| | (cm) | 10 | **10** | 11.5 | **12.5** | 14 | 14.5 |

## Gauge

18 sts x 10 rows over a 4in. (10cm) square working half double crochet using a F/5 (4mm) hook.

## Back

Using A and F/5 (4mm) hook, make 33:**37**:41:**45**:49:**53**ch.

**Row 1**: 1hdc in third ch from hook and in each ch to end. (31:**35**:39:**43**:47:**49** sts)

**Row 2**: 2ch, 1hdc in each st to end.

Rep Row 2 until work measures 6:**6**:7:**8**:8½:**9**in. (15:**15**:17.5:**20**:21.5:**22.5**cm).

Do not fasten off.

**Add sleeves to back:**

Make 16:**20**:24:**28**:32:**36**ch, turn.

**Row 1**: 1hdc in third ch from hook, 1hdc in each st across back to end of row, make 16:**20**:24:**28**:32:**36**ch for second sleeve, turn.

**Row 2**: 1hdc in third ch from hook, 1hdc in each st to end of row.

**Row 3**: 2ch, 1hdc in each st to end.

Rep Row 3 until a total of 12:**12**:14:**15**:17:**18** rows have been completed on right sleeve, 11:**11**:13:**14**:16:**17** rows on left sleeve.

Fasten off.

## Front (make left and right fronts the same)

Using A and F/5 (4mm) hook, make 17:**19**:21:**23**:25:**27**ch, turn.

**Row 1**: 1hdc in third ch from hook and in each ch to end. (15:**17**:19:**21**:23:**25** sts)

**Row 2**: 2ch, 1hdc in next and each st to end. Rep Row 2 and work as for back to underarm.

**Add sleeves to front:**

Make 16:**20**:24:**28**:32:**36**ch, turn.

**Next row**: 1hdc in third ch from hook, 1hdc in each st across front to end. (29:**35**:41:**47**:53:**59** sts)

**Next row**: 2ch, 1hdc in each st to end.

Rep last row until 8:**8**:8:**10**:10:**12** rows have been completed ending at sleeve edge.

**Neck shaping:**

**Next row**: 2ch, 1hdc across 23:**29**:34:**38**:43:**46** sts, leaving 6:**6**:7:**9**:10:**13** sts unworked.

**Next row**: 2ch, 1hdc in each st to sleeve edge. Rep last row twice more.

Fasten off.

When working on second front, start with RS facing and make sleeve ch at opposite end to first front.

With RS together, join shoulder seams with ss, working in back loops only.

**Sleeve cuffs:**

With RS facing, join yarn in first st, make 1ch, turn.

**Row 1**: 1sc in each row end along edge of sleeve. (23:**23**:27:**29**:33:**35** sts)

**Row 2**: 1ch, 1sc in next 2 sts, [sc2tog, 1sc in each of next 2:**2**:3:**3**:4:**4** sts] 5 times, 1sc in each st to end. (18:**18**:22:**24**:28:**30** sts)

**Row 3**: 1ch, 1sc in first and each st to end.

Rep last row 3 times more.

Fasten off.

With RS together, join side seams and sleeve seams.

## Buttonbands

**Left side:**

With RS facing, join yarn in top neck edge.

**Row 1**: 1ch, make 34:**34**:37:**40**:42:**44** sts along front edge.

**Row 2**: 1ch, 1sc in each st to end.

**Row 3 (buttonhole row)**: 1ch, 1sc in first st, *2ch, skip 2 sts, 1sc in each of next 5:**5**:6:**7**:7:**7** sts; rep from * 3 times more, 1sc in each st to end of row.

**Row 4**: 1ch, 1sc in each st to end, making 2sc in each buttonhole space.

**Row 5**: 1ch, 1sc in each st to end.

Fasten off.

**Right side:**

With RS facing, join yarn at bottom front edge.

**Row 1**: 1ch, make 34:**34**:37:**40**:42:**44** sts along front edge.

**Row 2**: 1ch, 1sc in each st to end. Rep Row 2 three times more.

Fasten off.

## Neck edging

With RS facing, join yarn with ss at right front edge.

1ch, 4sc across front band, 17:**17**:19:**21**:24:**27** sts across right front neck, 1sc in each st across back, 17:**17**:19:**21**:24:**27** sts across left neck, 4sc across front band.

**Next row**: 1ch, 1sc in each st around neck edge.

Rep last row once more.

Fasten off.

## Pocket

Using B and E/4 (3.5mm) hook, make 6ch, ss in first ch to form a ring.

**Round 1**: 3ch, dc2tog in ring *3ch, dc3tog in ring, 2ch, dc3tog in ring; rep from * twice more, 3ch, dc3tog in ring, 2ch ss in top of first 3-ch. Fasten off B.

**Round 2**: Join in C to any 3-ch sp, 3ch, dc2tog in same 3-ch sp, *3ch, dc3tog in same sp, 1ch, 3dc in next 2ch sp, 1ch, dc3tog in next 3-ch sp; rep from * twice more, 3ch, dc3tog in same sp, 1ch, 3dc in next 2-ch sp, 1ch, ss in top of first 3-ch. Fasten off C.

**Round 3**: Join in A into fasten off st, 1sc in top of first dc3tog from previous round, *3sc in corner ch sp, 1sc in top of next dc3tog from previous round, 1sc in next ch sp, 1sc in top of each of next 3 dc, 1sc in next ch sp, 1sc in top of next dc3tog from previous round; rep from * twice more. 3sc in corner ch sp, 1sc in top of next dc3tog from previous round, 1sc in next ch sp, 1sc in top of each of next 3 dc, 1sc in next ch sp, ss in first sc.

Fasten off.

## Finishing

Attach pocket to bottom of left front edge by sewing sides and bottom, leaving the top open for the pocket opening.

Sew in ends.

# Flower Power Cardigan

A very easy and sweet little cardigan, to suit even a newborn, this is a simple project that is suitable for beginners.

## Materials

**50% baby alpaca/50% merino light worsted (DK) yarn, such as Rooster Almerino Baby**

→ 1:2:3:3:4:5 x 1¾oz (50g) balls—approx. 136½:273:409½:409½:546:682½yds (125:250:375:375:500:625m)—of pale green (MC)

→ Scraps of lilac, white, dark pink, light pink, and mid-pink

→ D/3 (3mm) crochet hook

→ 3–6 buttons (depending on size)

## Abbreviations

**ch** chain; **dc** double crochet; **MC** main color; **rep** repeat; **sc** single crochet; **sc2tog** (single crochet 2 together decrease) insert hook in next st, yo, pull yarn through (2 loops on hook). Without finishing st, insert hook in next st, yo, pull yarn through (3 loops on hook), yo, pull yarn through all 3 loops on hook; **ss** slip stitch; **st(s)** stitch(es); **yo** yarn over hook

## Size

**To fit age**: Newborn:0–3:3–6:6–12:12–24:24–36

## Finished

| Chest | (in.): | 12 | 15 | 19 | 23 | 27 | 31 |
|---|---|---|---|---|---|---|---|
| | (cm): | 30 | 37.5 | 47.5 | 57.5 | 67.5 | 77.5 |
| Length | (in.): | 7 | 8½ | 10 | 11½ | 13 | 14½ |
| | (cm): | 17.5 | 21.5 | 25 | 29 | 32.5 | 36.5 |
| Sleeve seam | (in.): | 4½ | 5 | 6½ | 8 | 10 | 11 |
| | (cm): | 11.5 | 12.5 | 16.5 | 20 | 25 | 27.5 |

## Gauge

15 sts x 9 rows over a 4in. (10cm) square working double crochet using a D/3 (3mm) hook.

## Back and sides

Made in one piece starting at neck edge and working down from top.

Using MC, make 36:48:60:72:84:96ch.
**Row 1**: 1dc in fourth ch from hook, 1dc in each of next 3:5:7:9:11:13 ch, 3dc in next ch, 1dc in each of next 5:7:9:11:13:15 ch, 3dc in next ch, 1dc in each of next 10:14:18:22:26:30 ch, 3dc in next ch, 1dc in each of next 5:7:9:11:13:15 ch, 3dc in next ch, 1dc in each of last 5:7:9:11:13:15 ch.
**Rows 2–5**: 3ch, 1dc in each st, 3dc in top of middle st of each of 3-dc group of previous row.
**Row 6**: 3ch, 1dc in each st to middle of first 3-dc group. 1dc in top of 3-dc group, 4:5:6:7:8:9ch, skip each st of previous row to next 3-dc group, 1dc in top of middle st of 3-dc group and in each st across to middle of third 3-dc group, 4:5:6:7:8:9ch, skip each st of previous row to next 3-dc group, 1dc in top of middle st of 3-dc group and in each st to end.
**Row 7**: 3ch, 1dc in each st and 1dc in each ch along row to end.
**Rows 8–15:19:23:27:31:35**: 3ch, 1dc in each st to end, 2ch at end of last row.

## Edging

**Left front edge:**
Turn to work up left front edge.
**Row 1**: Work 25:30:35:40:45:50sc evenly up side of left front, 1ch, turn.
**Row 2**: 1sc in each st back down front, 1ch, turn.
**Row 3**: 1sc in each st, 1ch, turn.
**Row 4**: 1sc in each st to last st, 3sc in last st.
**Bottom edge:**
Work 1sc evenly along bottom edge, 3sc in last st.
**Right front edge:**
**Row 1**: Work 25:30:35:40:45:50sc evenly up side of right front, 1ch, turn

**Row 2**: 1sc in each st, 1ch, turn.

Place markers down right front edge at buttonhole positions.

**Buttonholes:**

**Row 3**: For each buttonhole: 1sc in each st to marker point, *skip 2 sts, 2ch, 1sc in each st to next marker point; rep from * to last buttonhole, 1sc in each st to end.

**Row 4**: 1ch, 1sc in each st to end, making 2sc in buttonhole ch sps, 3sc in last st.

Fasten off.

**Neck edge:**

Join yarn at top edge of right hand front, 1sc evenly around neck edge, making sc2tog after every fifth st to bring neck edge in.

Fasten off.

## Sleeves

Join yarn in center st at bottom of armhole.

**Round 1**: 3ch, 1dc in each st around armhole, join with a ss in top of first 3-ch.

**Rounds 2–8:9:12:16:22:24**: 3ch, 1dc in each dc, ss in top of first 3-ch.

**Round 9:10:13:17:23:25**: 1ch, 1sc in each st to end, ss in top of first ch.

Fasten off.

## Flowers

Using different color for each flower, make 4ch, ss in first ch to make a ring.

*3ch, 2dc in ring, 3ch, ss in ring; rep from * until 5 petals are made.

Fasten off leaving a long end.

Using long end in yarn needle weave around center to close circle.

Using contrast color, make French knot in center of each flower, wrapping wool around needle five times.

## Finishing

Sew on buttons.

Sew flowers around neck and bottom edge.

# Ship Ahoy Sweater

A bright and cheery striped sweater with an embroidered anchor. A very simple design made using half double crochet stitches.

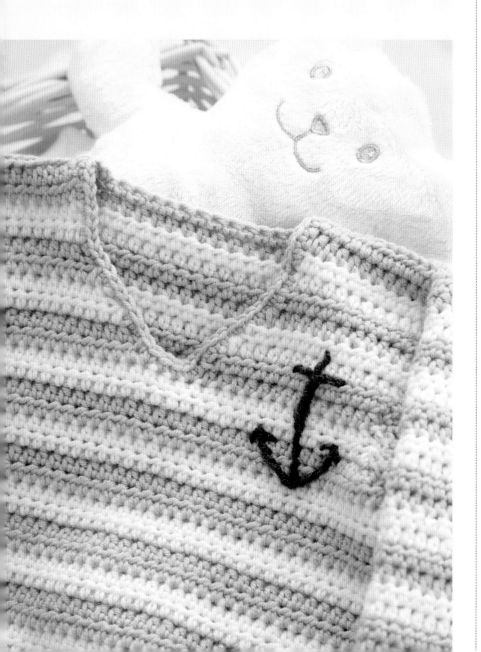

## Materials

**50% baby alpaca/50% merino light worsted (DK) yarn, such as Rooster Almerino Baby**

➔ 2:2:2:3 x 1¾oz (50g) balls—approx. 273:**273**:273:**409**½yds (250:**250**:250:**375**m)—each of aqua blue (A) and white (B)

➔ Scrap of dark blue

➔ D/3 (3mm) crochet hook

## Abbreviations

**ch** chain; **cont** continue; **rem** remaining; **rep** repeat; **RS** right side; **sc** single crochet; **ss** slip stitch; **st(s)** stitch(es); **WS** wrong side; **yo** yarn over hook

## Special abbreviation

**hdc2tog** (half double crochet 2 together decrease) *yo, insert hook in next st, yo, pull yarn through (3 loops on hook). Without finishing st, rep from * in next st (5 loops on hook), yo, pull yarn through all 5 loops on hook

## Size

**To fit age**: 3–6:**6–12**:12–18:**24–36** months

## Finished size

| Chest | (in.): | 20½ | 22½ | 24½ | 25½ |
|---|---|---|---|---|---|
| | (cm): | 51.5 | **56.5** | 61.5 | **64** |
| Length | (in.): | 12 | 12 | 13½ | 15½ |
| | (cm): | 30 | **30** | 34 | **39** |
| Sleeve seam | (in.): | 4½ | 4½ | 4½ | 5¾ |
| | (cm): | 11.5 | **11.5** | 11.5 | **14.5** |

## Gauge

18 sts x 15 rows over a 4in. (10cm) square working half double crochet using a D/3 (3mm) hook.

## Back

Alternate colors every second row throughout.

Using A, make 46:**50**:54:**58**ch.

**Row 1 (RS)**: 1hdc in third ch from hook, 1hdc in each ch to end. (44:**48**:52:**56** sts)

**Row 2**: 2ch, 1hdc in each st.

Join in B.

*Using B, rep Row 2 twice.

Using A, rep Row 2 twice.

Rep from * until work measures 7½:**7½**:8½:**9⅜**in. (19:**19**:21.5:**24**cm) ending with a RS row.

Fasten off.

**Armholes:**

**Row 1 (WS facing)**: Skip each of next 5 sts, join yarn into next st, 2ch, 1hdc into each of next 34:**38**:42:**46** sts, leaving last 5 sts unworked, turn. (34:**38**:42:**46** sts)**

Cont working straight until armhole measures 4½:**4½**:4½:**5¼**in. (11.5:**11.5**:11.5:**13**cm).

**Shoulders:**

**Next row**: 2ch, work 11:**12**:13:**14** sts.

Fasten off.

Skip next 12:**14**:16:**18** sts, rejoin yarn into next st, 2ch, 1hdc into each of rem 11:**12**:13:**14** sts.

Fasten off.

## Front

Work as for back until **.

**Next two rows**: 2ch, 1hdc into each st to end.

**Neck Side 1:**

**Row 1 (WS)**: 2ch, 1hdc in each of next 17:**19**:21:**23** sts. (17:**19**:21:**23** sts)

**Row 2**: 2ch, skip 1 st (neck edge), 1hdc in each st to end. (16:**18**:20:**22** sts)

**Row 3**: 2ch, 1hdc in each st to last 2 sts, hdc2tog (neck edge). (15:**17**:19:**21** sts)

Rep Rows 2 and 3 until 12:**13**:13:**14** sts rem. Work 2ch, 1hdc in each st to end until front measures same length as back.

**Neck Side 2:**

With WS facing, work Side 2 to match Side 1, reversing shaping.

Sew in all loose ends.

## Sleeves

Make 28:**28**:30:**32**ch.

1hdc in third ch from hook, 1hdc in each ch to end. (26:**26**:28:**30** sts)

**Rows 1–2**: 2ch, 1hdc in each st to end.

**Row 3**: 2ch, 2hdc into first st, 1hdc to last st, 2hdc in last st. (28:**28**:30:**32** sts)

**Row 4**: Rep Row 3. (30:**30**:32:**34** sts)

**Row 5**: Rep Row 3. (32:**32**:34:**36** sts)

Rep last 4 rows until there are 42:**42**:42:**46** sts.

Cont to work in hdc without increasing until work measures 7:**8**:9:**11**in. (17.5:**20**:22.5:**27.5**cm).

Fasten off.

## Finishing

Block pieces and steam gently.

Join shoulder seams.

With WS facing, place a pin marker at center of the top of sleeve. Pin sleeve at pin marker to shoulder seam and pin sleeve around armhole edge. Sew in place.

**Lower edging:**

With RS facing and using B, join yarn to lower edge at one of side seams, 1ch, work a round of sc evenly along lower edge. Ss into first ch to join round.

Fasten off, sew in ends.

**Neck edging:**

With RS facing, join yarn at neck edge of one of shoulder seams, 1ch, make 1sc evenly around neck edge, join with ss into first ch.

Fasten off.

Using scrap of dark blue, embroider an anchor onto top left-hand shoulder.

# Heart Tank Top

This is a really useful top; it's easy to slip on over a T-shirt and comfortable to wear. When crocheting intarsia, use separate balls of yarn for each side and join in the new color on the stitch before.

## Materials

**50% baby alpaca/50% merino mix light worsted (DK) yarn, such as Rooster Almerino DK**
→ 2:2:3:3 x 1¾oz (50g) balls—approx. 248:248:372:372yds (225:225:337.5:337.5m)—of light pink (A)
→ 1 x 1¾oz (50g) ball—approx. 124yds (112.5m)—of cream (B)
→ F/5 (4mm) crochet hook

## Abbreviations

**ch** chain; **cont** continue; **foll** following; **hdc** half double crochet; **rem** remaining; **rep** repeat; **RS** right side; **sc** single crochet; **ss** slip stitch; **st(s)** stitches; **WS** wrong side; **yo** yarn over hook

## Special abbreviation

**hdc2tog** (half double crochet 2 together decrease) *yo, insert hook in next st, yo, pull yarn through (3 loops on hook). Without finishing st, rep from * in next st (5 loops on hook), yo, pull yarn through all 5 loops on hook

## Size

**To fit age:** 3–6:6–12:12–18:24–36 months

## Finished size

|  | | | | | |
|---|---|---|---|---|---|
| Chest | (in.): | 21 | 22½ | 25 | 26 |
| | (cm): | 52.5 | 56.5 | 62.5 | 65 |
| Length | (in.): | 11½ | 12½ | 13 | 14½ |
| | (cm): | 29 | 31.5 | 32.5 | 36.5 |
| Armhole to shoulder | (in.): | 4 | 4½ | 4½ | 5 |
| | (cm): | 10 | 11.5 | 11.5 | 12.5 |

## Gauge

17 sts x 13 rows over a 4in. (10cm) square working half double crochet using a F/5 (4mm) hook.

## Back

Using A, make 47:**51**:55:**59**ch.
Row 1 (RS). 1hdc in third ch from hook, 1hdc in next and each ch to end. (45:**49**:53:**57** sts)
**Next row:** 2ch, 1hdc in each st.
Cont working straight until work is 24:**28**:28:**30** rows ending with a WS row.
    Fasten off.

**Armholes:**
Row 1 (RS facing): Skip 5 sts, join yarn in next st, 2ch, 1hdc in each of next 35:**39**:43:**47** sts, leaving last 5 sts unworked. (35:**39**:43:**47** sts)
    Cont working straight until armhole measures 4:**4½**:4½:**5**in. (10:**11.5**:11.5:**12.5**cm).

**Shoulders:**
**Next row:** 2ch, work 11:**12**:12:**13** sts.
    Fasten off.
    Skip next 13:**15**:15:**19** sts, rejoin yarn in next st, 2ch, 1hdc in each of rem 11:**12**:12:**13** sts.
    Fasten off.

## Front

Using A, make 47:**51**:55:**59**ch.
    Work first 3:**7**:7:**9** rows as back. (45:**49**:53:**57** sts)

**Heart motif:**
With WS facing, start with Row 1 of chart using Intarsia method and B for heart motif. First heart motif st is the 23rd:**25th**:25th:**27th**. Work with 2 separate balls of A when working from chart plus third ball for top indent in heart.
**Next row:** Using A, 2ch, 1hdc in each st to end.

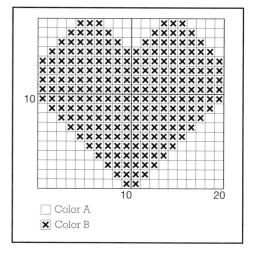

☐ Color A
☒ Color B

Fasten off.

**Armholes:**

**Row 1 (RS facing)**: Skip first 5 sts, rejoin yarn in next st, 2ch, 1hdc in each of next 35:**39**:43:**47** sts, leaving last 5 sts unworked, turn. (35:**39**:43:**47** sts)

**Rows 2–3**: 2ch, 1hdc in each st to end.

Divide for neck.

**Neck Side 1 (right neck edging):**

**Row 1 (WS facing)**: 2ch, 1hdc in each of foll 17:**19**:21:**23** sts, turn.

**Row 2**: 2ch, skip 1 st (neck edge), 1hdc in each st to end.

**Row 3**: 2ch, 1hdc in each st to last 2 sts, hdc2tog (neck edge). (15:**17**:19:**21** sts)

Rep Rows 2 and 3 until 11:**12**:12:**13** sts rem.

Work 2ch, 1hdc in each st to end until front measures same length as back.

Fasten off.

**Neck Side 2:**

With WS facing, skip 1 st at beginning of neck edge, rejoin yarn in next st.

**Row 1 (WS facing)**: 2ch, 1hdc in each of foll 17:**19**:21:**23** sts.

Work Side 2 to match Side 1, reversing shaping.

**Finishing**

Block pieces and steam gently. Join shoulder and side seams. Sew in ends.

**Lower edging:**

Using B and with RS facing, join yarn to lower edge at one of the side seams, 1ch, work a round of sc evenly along lower edge, ss in first ch to join round.

Fasten off.

**Neck edging:**

With RS facing join yarn at neck edge of one of the shoulder seams.

1ch, make 1sc evenly around neck edge, join with a ss in first ch.

Fasten off.

**Armhole edging:**

With RS facing, join yarn to top of one of the side seams, 1ch, work a round of sc evenly around armhole, join with a ss in first ch.

Fasten off.

Rep for second armhole.

# Pompom Cardigan

This is a really popular cardigan; pretty pompoms and a frill edge make it a cute baby garment. Don't make the pompoms too thick—loose and fluffy ones are much kinder on the neck.

## Materials

**50% baby alpaca/50% merino mix light worsted (DK) yarn, such as Rooster Almerino DK**

➜ 3:**3**:4:**4**:5:**5** x 1¾oz (50g) balls—approx. 372:**372**:496:**496**:620:**620**yds (337.5:**337.5**:450:**450**:562.5:**562.5**m)—of red (A)

➜ Scraps of off-white (B), light blue (C), orange (D), green (E), and blue (F)

➜ E/4 (3.5mm) crochet hook size

➜ 3 buttons

## Abbreviations

**ch** chain; **dc** double crochet; **hdc** half double crochet; **rep** repeat; **RS** right side; **sc** single crochet; **sc2tog** (single crochet 2 together decrease) insert hook in next st, yo, pull yarn through (2 loops on hook). Without finishing st, insert hook in next st, yo, pull yarn through (3 loops on hook), yo, pull yarn through all 3 loops on hook; **ss** slip stitch; **st(s)** stitch(es); **yo** yarn over hook

## Special abbreviation

**Shell** 1sc, skip 2 sts, 5dc in next st, skip 2 sts (1 shell made)

## Size

**To fit age:** 0–3:**3–6**:6–12:**12–18**:18–24:**24–36** months

## Finished size

| Chest | | | | | | | |
|---|---|---|---|---|---|---|---|
| | (in.): | 19 | 20½ | 25 | 26 | 27 | 28 |
| | (cm): | 47.5 | 51.5 | 62.5 | 65 | 67.5 | 70 |
| Length | (in.): | 10½ | 10½ | 11½ | 13 | 14 | 15 |
| | (cm): | 26.5 | 26.5 | 29 | 32.5 | 35 | 37.5 |
| Sleeve seam | (in.): | 4 | 4 | 4½ | 5 | 5½ | 5¾ |
| | (cm): | 10 | 10 | 11.5 | 12.5 | 14 | 14.5 |

## Gauge

16 sts x 10 rows over a 4in. (10cm) square working half double crochet using a E/4 (3.5mm) hook.

## Back

Using A, make 33:**37**:41:**45**:49:**53**ch.

**Row 1:** 1hdc in third ch from hook and each ch to end. (31:**35**:39:**43**:47:**49** sts)

**Row 2:** 2ch, 1hdc in each st to end.

Rep Row 2 until 20:**20**:24:**26**:26:**28** rows have been worked.

Do not fasten off.

**Add sleeves:**

Make 16:**20**:24:**28**:32:**36**ch, turn.

**Row 1:** 1hdc in third ch from hook, 1hdc in each st across the back to end of row, make 16:**20**:24:**28**:32:**36**ch for second sleeve, turn.

**Row 2:** 1hdc in third ch from hook, 1hdc in each st to end of row.

**Row 3:** 2ch, 1hdc in each st to end.

Rep Row 3 until a total of 12:**12**:14:**15**:17:**18** rows have been completed on right sleeve, 11:**11**:13:**14**:16:**17** rows on left sleeve.

Fasten off.

## Front (make left and right fronts the same)

Make 17:**19**:21:**23**:25:**27**ch, turn.

**Row 1:** 1hdc in third ch from hook and in each ch to end. (15:**17**:19:**21**:23:**25** sts)

**Row 2:** 2ch, 1hdc in each st to end.

Rep Row 2 and work as for back to underarm.

**Add sleeves:**

Make 16:**20**:24:**28**:32:**36**ch, turn.

**Next row:** 1hdc in third ch from hook, 1hdc in each st across front to end. (29:**35**:41:**47**:53:**59** sts)

**Next row:** 2ch, 1hdc in each st to end.

Rep last row until 8:**8**:8:**10**:10:**12** rows have been completed, ending at sleeve edge.

**Neck shaping:**

**Next row:** 2ch, 1hdc across 23:**29**:34:**38**:43:46 sts, leaving 6:**6**:7:**9**:10:13 sts unworked.

**Next row:** 2ch, 1hdc in each st to sleeve edge.

Rep last row twice more.

Fasten off.

When working on second front, start with RS facing and make sleeve ch at opposite end to first front.

With RS together, join shoulder seams with ss, working in back loops only.

**Sleeve cuffs:**

With RS facing, join yarn with ss in first st, make 1ch, turn.

**Row 1**: 1sc in each row end along edge of sleeve. (23:**23**:27:**29**:33:**35** sts)

**Row 2**: 1ch, 1sc in next 2 sts, [sc2tog, 1sc in each of next 2:**2**:3:**3**:4:**4** sts] 5 times, 1sc in each st to end. (18:**18**:22:**24**:28:**30** sts)

**Row 3**: 1ch, 1sc in first and each st to end.

Rep last row 3 times more.

Fasten off.

**Finishing**

With RS together, join side seams and sleeve seams.

Work shells to fit between markers. Adjust spacings between shells to either skip 1 st or 2 sts. Shells are either made in row ends or sts.

**Left front edge:**

Place marker halfway down left front edge and work shell edging down left front edge in row ends.

With RS facing, join yarn in first of 6 sts at neck edge of left front, work 4:**4**:4:**4**:5:**6** shells evenly along edge to marker, make another 3:**3**:4:**4**:4:**5** shells evenly to bottom edge, make 1 shell in corner stitch. (8:**8**:9:**9**:10:**11** shells)

**Bottom edge:**

Divide bottom edge into four by placing marker along bottom edge at each front/back seam and another marker in center of the back. (3 markers)

Make 3:**3**:4:**4**:5:**5** shells along front bottom edge to first marker, 6:**6**:7:**7**:8:**8** shells along back bottom edge to next marker, 2:**2**:3:**3**:4:**4**

shells along bottom right front edge and 1 shell in next corner. (12:**12**:15:**15**:18:**18** shells)

**Right front edge:**

Place marker halfway up right front edge. Working in row ends make 3:**3**:4:**4**:4:**5** shells evenly to marker. Make 3:**3**:4:**4**:4:**5** shells evenly to top edge, ending with a sc in last st. (7:**7**:8:**8**:9:**10** shells)

Fasten off. (27:**27**:32:**32**:37:**39** shells)

**Neck edging:**

**Row 1**: Join yarn in top of last dc made in shell, 1sc in same st, 1sc in each of next 7 sts, 8:**8**:9:**11**:12:**15** sc across right front neck to shoulder seam, 1sc in each of next 17:**17**:18:**22**:24:**30** sts across back, 8:**8**:9:**11**:12:**15** sc across left front neck, 1sc in each of next 7 sts, 1sc in top of first dc of shell, turn.

**Row 2**: 1ch, 1sc in first st, 1sc in each st around neck edge.

**Row 3**: Rep Row 2.

Fasten off.

Using B, C, D, E, F, make 12 (or enough to fit around neck edge) small and light pompoms (see page 65), making sure they are not too thick, and sew around collar.

Using shell holes as buttonholes, sew 3 buttons onto front edge.

# Trill-edged Cardigan

Something for a special occasion or when you want to go Hollywood and really dress up your baby. This is a really lovely, glamorous little cardigan and an easy pattern.

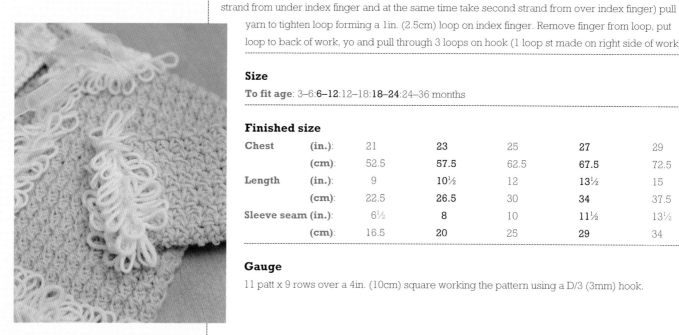

### Materials
50% baby alpaca/50% merino light worsted (DK) yarn, such as Rooster Almerino Baby
→ 3:3:3:4:5 x 1¾oz (50g) balls—approx. 409½:409½:409½:546:682½yds (375:375:375:500:625m) of pale green (A)
→ 1 x 1¾oz (50g) ball—approx. 124yds (112.5m)—of off-white (B)
→ D/3 (3mm) crochet hook
→ 40in (1m) cream ribbon, cut in half

### Abbreviations
**ch** chain; **beg** beginning; **patt(s)** pattern(s); **rep** repeat; **RS** right side; **sc** single crochet; **sp** space; **ss** slip stitch; **st(s)** stitch(es); **WS** wrong side; **yo** yarn over hook

### Special abbreviations
**Patt Row 1** (used on a foundation ch only) 1sc in second ch from hook, insert hook in same ch, pull yarn through (2 loops on hook), *skip 1ch, insert hook in next ch and pull yarn through (3 loops on hook), yo and pull through all 3 loops, 1ch (1 patt made), insert hook in same ch as last st, pull yarn through; rep from * ending with one complete patt, 1sc in last ch, 1ch, turn
**Patt Row 2** 1sc in first st, insert hook in ch sp between first st and first patt of last row, pull yarn through (2 loops on hook), *insert hook in ch sp after next patt from previous row, pull yarn through all 3 loops on hook, 1ch (1 patt made), insert hook in same sp as last st, pull yarn through; rep from * to last patt from previous row, work patt over last patt from previous row, 1sc in first sc of previous row, 1ch
**Loop st** *With yarn over left index finger, insert hook in next st, draw 2 strands through st (take first strand from under index finger and at the same time take second strand from over index finger) pull yarn to tighten loop forming a 1in. (2.5cm) loop on index finger. Remove finger from loop, put loop to back of work, yo and pull through 3 loops on hook (1 loop st made on right side of work)

### Size
**To fit age:** 3–6:**6–12**:12–18:**18–24**:24–36 months

### Finished size
| Chest | (in.): | 21 | 23 | 25 | 27 | 29 |
|---|---|---|---|---|---|---|
| | (cm): | 52.5 | 57.5 | 62.5 | 67.5 | 72.5 |
| Length | (in.): | 9 | 10½ | 12 | 13½ | 15 |
| | (cm): | 22.5 | 26.5 | 30 | 34 | 37.5 |
| Sleeve seam | (in.): | 6½ | 8 | 10 | 11½ | 13½ |
| | (cm): | 16.5 | 20 | 25 | 29 | 34 |

### Gauge
11 patt x 9 rows over a 4in. (10cm) square working the pattern using a D/3 (3mm) hook.

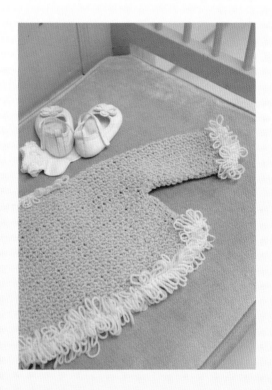

## Back

Using A and starting at lower edge, make 56:**66**:76:**86**:96ch.

**Row 1**: Work Patt Row 1 to complete 27:**32**:37:**42**:47 patts.

Work using Patt Row 2 until piece measures 5½:**6½**:8:**9**:10in. (14:**16.5**:20:**22.5**:25cm)

### Divide for sleeves:

Make 32:**38**:44:**50**:56ch for first sleeve.

Drop loop off hook, do not fasten off.

With RS facing, join a separate ball of A in sc at opposite end of last row, make 32:**38**:44:**50**:56ch for second sleeve.

Fasten off.

Pick up dropped loop, turn.

Work Patt Row 1 on 32:**38**:44:**50**:56ch to complete 15:**18**:21:**24**:27 patts, draw up a loop in same ch as last st, skip last ch and 1 sc, draw up a loop between sc and first patt, yo and through 3 loops on hook, 1ch.

Work in patt across back to last sc, insert hook in same sp as last pattern, skip 1 st, draw up a loop in first ch of 32:**38**:44:**50**:56ch, yo and pull through all 3 loops on hook, 1ch.

Work 15:**18**:21:**24**:27 patts across ch, 1sc in last ch (59:**65**:71:**77**:83 patts), 1ch, turn.

Work in patt until sleeves measure 3½:**3½**:4:**4**:4½in. (9:**9**:10:**10**:11.5cm) straight up from sleeve ch, 1ch, turn.

### Right shoulder and front:

Work 24:**27**:29:**32**:34 patts, 1sc in same sp as last st, 1ch, turn.

Work 2 more rows of 24:**27**:29:**32**:34 patts for shoulder.

Make 9:**13**:17:**19**:25ch for front, turn.

Work 4:**6**:8:**10**:12 patts on chain, plus 1 patt over sc at neck edge.

Continue across front and sleeve in patt. (29:**31**:33:**35**:37 patts)

*Work across 29:**31**:33:**35**:37 patts until sleeve measures 3½:**4**:4½:**5**:5½in. (9:**10**:11.5:**12.5**:14cm) from top of shoulder ending center front edge, 1ch, turn.

Work across 14:**16**:19:**21**:24 patts for front, 1sc in same sp as last st, 1ch, turn.

Work across 14:**16**:19:**21**:24 patts until front measures same as back to sleeve.

Fasten off.*

### Left shoulder and front:

Skip 11:**11**:13:**13**:15 patts for back of neck on last row of 59:**65**:71:**77**:83 patts.

Join A in sp before next patt, 1ch, 1sc in same sp.

Work in patt on next 24:**27**:29:**32**:34 patts to end of row.

Work 2 more rows of 24:**27**:29:**32**:34 patts, ending at sleeve edge.

Drop loop off hook, do not fasten off.

Join a separate ball of A at neck edge (beg of last row), make 8:**12**:16:**20**:24ch.

Fasten off.

Pick up loop at sleeve edge, 1ch, turn.

Work across 24:**27**:29:**32**:34 patts, work 1 patt over sc at neck edge, work 4:**6**:8:**10**:12 patts on 8:**12**:16:**20**:24ch. (29:**31**:33:**35**:37 patts)

Working from * to *, complete left front as for right front.

Sew side and sleeve seams.

## Frill edging

**Front and bottom edging:**

**Row 1**: With RS facing, join B at beg of left front neck edge, work 2sc in each row end along front edge, 3sc in corner, 2sc in each patt along bottom edge, 3sc in next corner, 2sc in each row end along right front edge, 3sc in corner of neck, 1sc in each patt st along right neck edge, finishing at left front neck edge, 1ch, turn.

**Row 2**: With WS facing, work Loop st in each st around neck, right front, bottom edge, left front, 1ch, turn.

Fasten off.

**Row 3**: With WS facing, join yarn in first st in right front neck edge, rep Row 2 along right front edge, bottom and up left front edge, finishing at top of left front edge.

Fasten off.

## Cuffs

**Round 1**: With RS facing, join B to cuff edge of sleeve at underarm seam, work 30sc around cuff edge evenly, ss in first sc to join round, turn.

**Round 2 (WS facing)**: 1ch, work Loop st in each st, join with a ss in first 1-ch, do not turn.

**Round 3**: 1ch, rep Round 2 to end, ss in first 1-ch.

Fasten off.

## Finishing

Block cardigan. Sew in ends.

Sew ribbon lengths on either side of neck edge for ties.

 Enthusiast

# Strawberry Kisses Sweater

A very appealing pattern; this is a warm garment made using a very soft alpaca/merino wool. When working the pattern rows, place markers in first and last stitches to help you keep track.

## Materials

**50% baby alpaca/50% merino mix light worsted (DK) yarn, such as Rooster Almerino DK**

→ 4:4:5:5:6:7 x 1¾oz (50g) balls—approx. 496:**496**:620:**620**:744:**868**yds (450:**450**:562.5:**562.5**:675:**787.5**m)—of yellow (A)

→ 1 x 1¾oz (50g) ball—approx. 124yds (112.5m)—of red (B)

→ Small amount of off-white (C) and green (D)

→ E/4 (3.5mm) and D/4 (3mm) crochet hooks

→ 1 button

## Abbreviations

**ch** chain; **dc** double crochet; **dec** decrease; **hdc** half double crochet; **inc** increase; **patt** pattern; **rep** repeat; **RS** right side; **sc** single crochet; **ss** slip stitch; **st(s)** stitch(es); **WS** wrong side; **yo** yarn over hook

## Special abbreviations

**Patt A** (Row 1 of patt, worked over 5 sts from right to left) Skip 1 st, 1dc in each of next 2 sts, placing hook in front of 2 dc just worked, yo, insert hook in skipped st (from WS to RS), yo, pull yarn through (3 loops on hook), yo, pull yarn through 2 loops, yo, pull yarn through a loop—this is the loop you catch on the next row—(2 loops on hook), yo, insert hook in fifth st, yo, pull yarn through (4 loops on hook), yo, pull yarn through 2 loops, yo, pull yarn through all 3 loops. Turn work to WS facing, 1 dc in each of third and fourth sts working from back, hook direction front to back

**Patt B** (Row 2 of patt, worked over 5 sts from right to left) Skip each of next 2 sts, 1dc in third st catching loop from previous row (where central cross is made), keeping hook in front of dc just worked make 1dc in first skipped st (from RS to WS), yo, insert hook in second skipped st (from front to back), yo, pull yarn through (3 loops on hook), yo, pull yarn through 2 loops (2 loops on hook), yo, insert hook in fourth st, yo, pull yarn through (4 loops on hook), yo, pull yarn through 2 loops, yo, pull yarn through 3 loops, 1dc in fifth st. Turn work to RS facing. To make fourth point of the cross, 1dc in third st, picking up central loop as before (where central cross is made), turn work back to WS facing

**dc2tog** (double crochet 2 together decrease) *yo, insert hook in next st, yo, pull yarn through, yo, pull yarn through 2 loops on hook (2 loops on hook). Without finishing st, rep from * in next st (3 loops on hook), yo, pull yarn through all 3 loops on hook

**dc2tog extra** (sts used will vary when decreasing) yo, insert hook in first st from back to front, yo, pull yarn through (3 loops on hook), yo, pull yarn through 2 loops, yo, pull yarn through 1 loop—this is the loop you catch on the next row—(2 loops on hook), yo, insert hook in fifth st, yo, pull yarn through, yo pull yarn through 2 loops, yo pull yarn through all 3 loops

**dc2tog over** (sts used will vary when decreasing) yo, insert hook in second st 2 from front to back, yo, pull yarn through (3 loops on hook), yo, pull yarn through 2 loops (2 loops on hook), yo, insert hook in fourth st, yo, pull yarn through (4 loops on hook), yo, pull yarn through 2 loops, yo, pull yarn through all 3 loops

## Size

**To fit age:** 0–3:**3–6**:6–12:**12–18**:18–24:**24–36** months

## Finished size

| Chest | (in.): | 20 | **22** | 24 | **26** | 28 | **30** |
|---|---|---|---|---|---|---|---|
| | (cm): | 50 | **55** | 60 | **65** | 70 | **75** |
| Length | (in.): | 13 | **15** | 17 | **19** | 21 | **23** |
| | (cm): | 32.5 | **37.5** | 42.5 | **47.5** | 52.5 | **57.5** |
| Sleeve | (in.): | 5 | **6½** | 8 | **10** | 11 | **12** |
| seam | (cm): | 12.5 | **16.5** | 20 | **25** | 27.5 | **30** |

## Gauge

2¾ patterns x 10 rows over a 4in. (10cm) square using a E/4 (3.5mm) hook.

## Back

Using E/4 (3.5mm) hook and A, make
50:**55**:60:**65**:70:**75**ch.

**Row 1:** 1sc in second ch from hook, 1sc in
each chain to end. (49:**54**:59:**64**:69:**74** sts)

**Row 2:** 1sc in first st, 1ch (counts as 1hdc),
1hdc in each st to end.

**Row 3 (row 1 of pattern):** 1sc in first st, 2ch
(counts as 1dc), 1dc in each of next 3 sts, *Patt
A, 1dc in each of next 4 sts; rep from * to end.

**Row 4 (row 2 of pattern):** 1sc in first st, 2ch
(counts as 1dc), 1dc in each of next 3 sts, *Patt
B, 1dc in each of next 4 sts; rep from * to end.

Rep Rows 3–4 another 8:**10**:12:**14**:16:**18**
times more.

### Shape for armholes:

**Row** 21:**25**:29:**33**:37:**41**: Ss in first 3 sts, 1sc in
next st, 2ch (counts as dc), Patt A, *1dc in
each of next 4 sts, Patt A; rep from * to last 4
sts, 1dc in next st, turn. (43:**48**:53:**58**:63:**68** sts)

**Row** 22:**26**:30:**34**:38:**42** (dec row Patt B): 1sc
in first st, 2ch (counts as 1dc), skip next 2 sts,
1dc in third st catching loop from previous
row (where central cross is made), keeping
hook in front of dc just worked dc2tog using
first and second sts (inserting hook from RS to
WS), dc2tog using fourth and fifth sts. Turn
work to RS facing. To make fourth point of
cross 1dc in third st picking up central loop
as before (where central cross is made), turn
work back to WS facing, 1dc in each of next
4 sts, *Patt B, 1dc in each of next 4 sts; rep
from * to last 6 sts, skip first and second sts,
1dc in third st catching loop from previous
row (where central cross is made). Keeping
hook in front of dc just worked dc2tog using
first and second sts (inserting hook from RS to

WS), dc2tog using fourth and fifth sts, turn work to RS facing. To make fourth point of cross 1dc in third st picking up central loop as before (where central cross is made). Turn work back to WS facing, 1dc in last st. (41:**46**:51:**56**:61:**66** sts)

**Row 23**:**27**:**31**:**35**:39:**43** (dec row, Patt A worked on 4 sts): 1sc in first st, 2ch (counts as 1dc), skip 3 sts, 1dc in next st, turn work to WS facing, 1 dc in each of first and second sts, turn work to RS facing, 1dc in each of next 4 sts, *Patt A, 1dc in each of next 4 sts; rep from * to last 5 sts, skip first st, 1dc in second st, dc2tog extra using first st and fourth st, turn work to WS facing, 1dc in third st, turn work to RS facing, 1dc in last st. (39:**44**:49:**54**:59:**64** sts)

**Row 24**:**28**:**32**:**36**:**40**:**44** (dec row, Patt B worked on 3 sts): 1sc in first st, 1ch, skip 1 st, 1dc in third st (counts as 1dc), turn work to RS facing, 1dc in second st, *1dc in each of next 4 sts, Patt B; rep from * to last 4 sts, skip first 2 sts, 1dc in third st (no extra loop to catch this time), dc2tog over using first and last st. (37:**42**:47:**52**:57:**62** sts)

**Row 25**:**29**:**33**:**37**:**41**:**45** (dec row): 1sc in first st, 2ch (counts as 1dc), dc2tog, 1dc in each of next 4 sts, *Patt A, 1dc in each of next 4 sts; rep from * to last 7 sts, 1dc in each of next 4 sts, dc2tog, 1dc in last st. (35:**40**:45:**50**:55:**60** sts)

**Row 26**:**30**:**34**:**38**:**42**:**46**: 1sc in first st, 2ch (counts as 1dc), 1dc in each of next 5 sts, *Patt B, 1dc in each of next 4 sts; rep from * to last 2 sts, 1dc in each of next 2 sts.

**Row 27**:**31**:**35**:**39**:**43**:**47**: 1sc in first st, 2ch (counts as 1dc), 1dc in each of next 5 sts, *Patt A, 1dc in each of next 4 sts; rep from *to last

2 sts, 1dc in each of next 2 sts.

**Row 28**:**32**:**36**:**40**:**44**:**48**: Rep Row 26:**30**:**34**:**38**:**42**:**46**.

**Row 29**:**33**:**37**:**41**:**45**:**49**: Rep Row 27:**31**:**35**:**39**:**43**:**47**.

**Row 30**:**34**:**38**:**42**:**46**:**50**: Rep Row 26:**30**:**34**:**38**:**42**:**46**.

Rep Rows 27–26 another 0:**1**:2:**3**:4:**4** times.

**Right shoulder:**

**Rows 31–33**:**36–38**:**40–42**:**46–48**:**52–54**:**58–60**: 1sc in first st, 2ch, 1dc in each of next 5:**7**:9:**11**:13:**15** sts.

Fasten off.

**Left shoulder (incl flap over):**

**Row 31**:**36**:**40**:**46**:**52**:**58**: With RS facing, join yarn with ss, 2ch in 6th:**8th**:10th:**12th**:14th:**16th** st from outside edge, 1dc in each of next 5:**7**:9:**11**:13:**15** sts, turn.

**Rows 32–36**:**37–41**:41–45:**49–51**:52–56:**58–62**: 1sc in first st, 2ch (counts as 1dc), 1dc in each of next 5:**7**:9:**11**:13:**15** sts.

Fasten off.

## Front

Work as Back to Row 25:**29**:31:**35**:39:**43**.

**Right front neck:**

**Row 26**:**30**:**32**:**36**:**40**:**44** (dec row Patt B): 1sc in first st, 2ch (counts as 1dc), 1dc in each of next 5 sts, Patt B, 1dc in next 1:**3**:5:**7**:9:**11** sts (neck edge), turn. (12:**14**:16:**18**:20:**22** sts)

**Row 27**:**31**:**33**:**37**:**41**:**45** (dec row Patt A): 1sc in first 1:**3**:5:**7**:9:**11** sts, 2ch (counts as 1dc), skip next st, dc2tog using second and third sts, keeping hook in front of dc just worked, dc2tog extra using first and fifth sts, turn work to WS facing, 1dc in each of third and fourth

sts, 1dc in each of next 6 sts. (11:**13**:15:**17**:19:**21** sts)

**Row 28**:**32**:**34**:**38**:**42**:**46** (dec row Patt B): 1sc in first st, 2ch (counts as 1dc), 1dc in each of next 5 sts, skip 2 sts, 1dc in next st catching loop from previous row, 1dc in first st, dc2tog over using second and fourth sts, turn work to RS facing. To make fourth point of cross 1dc in third st picking up central loop as before (where central cross is made), turn work back to WS facing, 1dc in each st to end. (10:**12**:14:**16**:18:**20** sts)

**Row 29**:**33**:**35**:**39**:**43**:**47** (dec row Patt A): 1sc in first st, 2ch (counts as 1dc), skip 2 sts, 1dc in next 1:**3**:5:**7**:9:**11** sts, turn work to WS facing, dc2tog using first and second sts, 1dc in each of next 6 sts. (9:**11**:13:**15**:17:**19** sts)

**Row 30**:**34**:**36**:**40**:**44**:**48**: 1sc in first st, 2ch, 1dc in each of next 5 sts, dc2tog, 1 dc in last st. (8:**10**:12:**14**:16:**18** sts)

**Row 31**:**35**:**37**:**41**:**45**:**49**: 1sc in first st, 2ch, dc2tog, 1dc in each of next 5 sts. (7:**9**:11:**13**:15:**17** sts)

**Row 32**:**36**:**38**:**42**:**46**:**50**: 1sc in first st, 2ch, 1dc in each of next 4 sts, dc2tog, 1dc in each st to end. (6:**8**:10:**12**:14:**16** sts)

**Row 33**:**37**:**39**:**43**:**47**:**51**: 1sc in first st, 2ch, 1dc in each st to end. (6:**8**:10:**12**:14:**16** sts)

Fasten off.

**Left front neck:**

With WS facing, join yarn in 12th:**14th**:16th:**18th**:20th:**22nd** st from left.

**Row 26**:**30**:**32**:**36**:**40**:**44** (dec row Patt B): 3ch (counts as 1:**3**:5:**7**:9:**11**dc), Patt B, 1dc in each of next 6 sts. (12:**14**:16:**18**:20:**22** sts)

**Row 27**:**31**:**33**:**37**:**41**:**45** (dec row Patt A): 1sc in first st, 2ch (counts as 1dc), 1dc in each of next 5 sts, skip 1 st, 1dc in each of second and third sts, keeping hook in front of dc just worked, dc2tog extra using first and fifth sts, turn work to WS facing, 1dc in third st, dc2tog over using fourth and last st. (11:**13**:15:**17**:19:**21** sts)

**Row 28:32:34:38:42:46 (dec row Patt B)**: 1sc in first st, 2ch (counts as 1dc), skip 1 st, 1dc in second st catching loop from previous row, dc2tog over using first and fourth sts, turn work to RS facing. To make fourth point of cross 1dc in second st picking up central loop as before (where central cross is made), turn work back to WS facing, 1dc in each of next 6 sts. (10:**12**:14:**16**:18:**20** sts)

**Row 29:33:35:39:43:47 (dec row Patt A)**: 1sc in first st, 2ch (counts as 1dc), 1dc in each of next 5 sts, dc2tog extra using first and third sts, turn work to WS facing, 1dc in first st, dc2tog over using second and last st. (9:**11**:13:**15**:17:**19** sts)

**Row 30:34:36:40:44:48**: 1sc in first st, 2ch, dc2tog, 1dc in each of next 6 sts. (8:**10**:12:**14**:16:**18** sts)

**Row 31:35:37:41:45:49**: 1sc in first st, 2ch (counts as 1dc), dc2tog, 1dc in each st to end. (7:**9**:11:**13**:15:**17** sts)

**Row 32:36:38:42:46:50**: 1sc in first st, 2ch, dc2tog, 1dc in each of next 4 sts. (6:**8**:10:**12**:14:**16** sts)

**Row 33:37:39:43:47:51**: 1sc in first st, 2ch, 1dc in each st to end. (6:**8**:10:**12**:14:**16** sts)
Fasten off.

## Sleeves (make 2)

Using E/4 (3.5mm) hook and A, make 28:**30**:32:**34**:36:**38**ch.

**Row 1**: 1sc in second ch from hook, 1sc in each ch to end.

**Row 2**: 1sc in first st, 1ch (counts as 1hdc), 1hdc in each st to end.

**Row 3**: 1sc in first st, 2ch (counts as 1dc), 1dc in next 1:**2**:3:**4**:5:**6** sts, Patt A, *1dc in each of next 4 sts, Patt A; rep from * once more, 1dc in each of last 2:**3**:4:**5**:6:**7** sts.

**Row 4**: 1sc in first st, 2ch (counts as 1dc), 1dc in next 1:**2**:3:**4**:5:**6** sts, Patt B, *1dc in each of next 4 sts, Patt B; rep from * once more, 1dc in each of last 2:**3**:4:**5**:6:**7** sts.

**Inc rows:**

**Row 5**: 1sc in first st, 2ch (counts as 1dc), 2dc in next st, 1dc in each of next 0:**1**:2:**3**:4:**5** sts, *Patt A, 1dc in each of next 4 sts; rep from * once more, Patt A, 1dc in each st to end.

**Row 6**: 1sc in first st, 2ch (counts as 1dc), 2dc in next st, 1dc in each of next 0:**1**:2:**3**:4:**5** sts, *Patt B, 1dc in each of next 4 sts; rep from * once more, Patt B, 1dc in each st to end.

**Rows 7–16**: Rep Rows 5–6 until there are 8:**9**:10:**11**:12:**13** dc at end of each row.

**Row 17**: 1ss in each of first 3 sts, 1sc in next 1:**2**:3:**4**:5:**6** sts, 2ch (counts as 1dc), 1dc in each of next 4 sts, Patt A, *1dc in each of next 4 sts, Patt A; rep from * once more, 1dc in each of next 5:**6**:7:**8**:9:**10** sts, turn.

Work 0:**4**:8:**12**:16:**20** rows without shaping.

**Dec rows:**

**Row 18:22:26:30:34:38**: 1sc in first st, 2ch (counts as 1dc), dc2tog, 1dc in each of next 2 sts, Patt B, *1dc in each of next 4 sts; rep from * once more, 1dc in each of next 2 sts, dc2tog, 1dc in last st.

**Row 19:23:27:31:35:39**: 1sc in first st, 2ch (counts as 1dc), dc2tog, 1dc in next st, Patt A,

*1dc in each of next 4 sts, Patt A; rep from * once more, 1dc in next st, dc2tog, 1dc in last st.

**Row 20:24:28:32:36:40**: 1sc in first st, 2ch (counts as 1dc), dc2tog, Patt B, *1dc in each of next 4 sts, Patt B; rep from * once more, dc2tog, 1dc in last st.

**Row 21:25:29:33:37:41**: 1sc in first st, [1ch, 1dc] (counts as dc2tog) Patt A, *1dc in each of next 4 sts, Patt A; rep from * once more, dc2tog.

**Row 22:26:30:34:38:42**: 1sc in first st, 2ch (counts as 1dc), Patt B, *1dc in each of next 4 sts, Patt B; rep from * once more, 1dc in last st.

**Row 23:27:31:35:39:43**: 1sc in first st, 2ch (counts as 1dc), Patt A, *1dc in each of next 4 sts, Patt A; rep from * once more, 1dc in last st.

**Row 24:28:32:36:40:44**: 1sc in first st, 2ch (counts as 1dc), Patt B, *1dc in each of next 4 sts, Patt B; rep from * once more, 1dc in last st.

**Row 25:29:33:37:41:45**: 1sc in first st, 2ch (counts as 1dc), skip next st, dc2tog using second and third sts, keeping hook in front of dc just worked dc2tog extra using first and fifth sts, turn work to WS facing, 1dc in third and fourth sts, 1dc in next st, dc2tog, 1dc in next st, Patt A, skip 1 st, 1dc in second and third sts, keeping hook in front of dc just worked, dc2tog extra using first and fifth sts, turn work to WS facing, dc2tog using third and fourth sts, 1dc in last st.
Fasten off.

## Finishing

With RS together, sew front and back together (left shoulder has more rows for button flap).
Sew sleeve seams.

**Neck edge:**
With RS facing, join yarn at left front shoulder edge, 2ch, 1hdc in each st (picking up even number of sts on both sides of neck edge). Work to position of buttonhole, 2ch, skip 2 sts, continue in hdc to end, turn, 1ch, 1sc in first st, 1sc in each st to end.

Sew button in place.

**Strawberries (make enough to go around bottom edge between crosses)**
Using D/4 (3mm) hook and B, make 2ch, 1sc in second ch from hook, 1ch, turn and make next row on side edge.

2sc in first st, 1ch, turn. (2 sts)

2sc in each st, 1ch, turn. (4 sts)

1sc in next st, 2sc in next st, 1sc in next st, 2sc in next st, 1ch, turn. (6 sts)

1sc in first st, 2sc in next st, 1sc in each of next 2 sts, 2sc in next st, 1sc in next st. (8 sts)

Fasten off leaving a long tail.

Fold sides together and hand sew along side and top of strawberry, folding and sewing in tip to neaten. Sew in ends.

Using yarn needle and C, embroider 3 small seeds on each strawberry.

**Leaves (make 1 for each strawberry)**
With RS facing and using D/4 (3mm) hook and D, insert hook through top sts (second from right) at top right side of strawberry and join yarn.

*Make 3ch, ss to base of ch, ss in next st; rep from * once more.

Fasten off. Sew in ends.

Sew strawberries around bottom edge between crosses.

CHAPTER TWO
# Stepping Out

# Lilac Bootees

The cutest little slippers with a strap to keep them in place.

### Materials

**50% baby alpaca/50% merino light worsted (DK) yarn, such as Rooster Almerino Baby**

→ 1 x 1¾oz (50g) ball—136yds (125m)   of purple (A) and lilac (B)

→ 2 buttons

→ D/3 (3mm) crochet hook

### Abbreviations

**ch** chain; **dc** double crochet; **hdc** half double crochet; **rep** repeat; **sc** single crochet; **sp** space; **ss** slip stitch; **st(s)** stitch(es)

### Size

**To fit age**: Newborn baby

### Finished size

**Length**: approx. 3½in. (9cm)

## Bootee (make 2)

Using A, make 12ch.

**Round 1**: 1sc in second ch from hook, 1sc in each of next 9ch, 6sc in last ch.

Working on other side of chain, 1sc in each ch to last ch, 2sc in last ch, join with ss in first st.

**Round 2**: 1ch, 1sc in each of next 6 sts, 1hdc in each of next 5 sts, *2hdc in next st, 1hdc in next st; rep from * once more, 2hdc in next st, 1hdc in each of next 5 sts, 1sc in each of next 7 sts, join with ss in first ch.

**Round 3**: 1ch, 1sc in next st, 2sc in next st, 1sc in each of next 4 sts, 1hdc in each of next 6 sts, *2hdc in next st, 1hdc in next st; rep from * twice more, 2hdc in next st, 1hdc in each of next 6 sts, 1sc in each of next 4 sts, 2sc in next st, 1sc in next st, 2sc in last st, join with ss in first ch.

**Round 4**: 2ch, 2hdc in next st, 1hdc in each of next 16 sts, *2hdc in next st, 1hdc in next st; rep from * once more, 2hdc in next st, 1hdc in each of next 16 sts, 2hdc in next st, 1hdc in last st, join with ss in top of first ch.

Join in B, do not fasten off A.

**Round 5**: Using B, 2ch, 1hdc in each st to end, join with ss in top of first ch.

Fasten off B.

**Round 6**: Using A, 1ch, 1sc in each st to end, ss in top of first ch, turn.

**Begin working in rows:**

**Row 1**: 1ch, skip first st, 1sc in next st, skip 1 st, 1sc in each of next 14 sts, *skip 1 st, 1sc in each of next 4 sts; rep from * twice more, skip 1 st, 1sc in each of next 14 sts, skip 1 st, join with ss in top of first ch.

**Row 2**: 1ch, 1sc in each of next 14 sts, *skip 1 st, 1sc in each of next 3 sts; rep from * twice more, skip 1 st, 1sc in each st to end.

**Row 3**: 1ch, 1sc in each of next 15 sts, *skip 1 st, 1sc in each of next 4 sts; rep from * once

more, skip 1 st, 1sc in each st to end.

Place a marker st in the center front st.

**Left-hand side:**

**Row 1**: 1ch, 1sc in each st to center point, skip center st, turn.

**Row 2**: 1ch, skip 1 st, 1sc in each st to end, turn.

**Row 3**: 1ch, 1sc in each st to last 4 sts, skip 1 st, 1sc in next st, skip 1 st, 1sc in last st, turn.

**Row 4**: 1ch, skip 1 st, 1sc in each st to

end, turn.

**Row 5**: 1ch, 1sc in each st to last 2 sts, skip 1 st, 1sc in last st, turn.

**Row 6**: 1ch, skip 1 st, 1sc in each st to end, turn.

**Row 7**: 1ch, 1sc in each st to end.

Fasten off.

**Right-hand side:**

Join A to st next to center front (do not use center stitch).

**Row 1**: 1ch, 1sc in each st, join with ss to center back, turn.

**Row 2**: 1ch, 1sc in each st to last 4 sts, skip 1 st, 1sc, skip 1 st, 1sc, turn.

**Row 3**: 1ch, skip 1 st, 1sc in next st, 1sc in each st to end, turn.

**Row 4**: 1ch, 1sc in each st to last 2 sts, skip 1 st, 1sc in last st, turn.

**Row 5**: 1ch, skip 1 st, 1sc in each st to end, turn.

**Rows 6–7**: 1ch, 1sc in each st to end.

Fasten off.

Join B in center back st, work 1sc around edge of bootee opening including center front stitch.

Fasten off.

## Straps (make 2)

Using A, make 11ch.

**Row 1**: 1sc in second ch from hook, 1sc in each st to end, turn.

**Row 2**: 1ch, 1sc in each st to end.

**Row 3**: 1ch, 1sc in each of next 7 sts, 2ch, skip 2 sts, 1sc in each st to end.

**Row 4**: 1ch, 1sc in each st (including 1sc in 2-ch) to end.

Fasten off.

## Finishing

Sew strap on left for right bootee and on right for left bootee.

Sew on buttons to match straps.

Beginner

# Ribbon Hat

This is a perfect first baby hat. It's so easy to make and the ribbon and flower add a delicate and stylish look.

## Materials

**50% baby alpaca/50% merino light worsted (DK) yarn, such as Rooster Almerino Baby**

→ 1 x 1¾oz (50g) ball—approx. 136yds (125m)—of off-white (A)
→ Small amount of lilac (B)
→ Small amount of purple (C)
→ D/3 (3mm) crochet hook
→ Approx. 12in. (30cm) of ½in. (1cm) wide lilac ribbon

## Abbreviations

**ch** chain; **dc** double crochet; **hdc** half double crochet; **rep** repeat; **sc** single crochet; **sp** space; **ss** slip stitch; **st(s)** stitch(es)

## Size

**To fit age**: Newborn baby

## Finished size

**Circumference**: 15in. (37.5cm)

## Gauge

24 sts x 15 rows over a 4in. (10cm) square working pattern using a D/3 (3mm) hook.

## Hat

Using A, make 4ch, ss in first ch to form a ring.
**Round 1**: 5ch, *1dc, 2ch in ring; rep from * 4 more times, ss in third of 5-ch, ss in fourth of same 5-ch.
**Round 2**: 5ch, *1dc in first ch sp, 2ch, *[1dc, 2ch, 1dc] in next ch sp; rep from * to end, ss in third of first 5-ch, ss in fourth of same 5-ch.
**Round 3**: 5ch, 1dc in first ch sp, *2ch, 1dc in next ch sp, 2ch, [1dc, 2ch, 1dc] in next ch sp; rep from * to end, ss in third of 5-ch, ss in fourth of same 5-ch.
**Round 4**: 5ch, 1dc in first ch sp, *2ch, 1dc in next ch sp, 2ch, 1dc in next ch sp. 2ch, [1dc, 2ch, 1dc] in next ch sp; rep from * to end, ss in third of 5-ch, ss in fourth of same 5-ch.
**Round 5**: 5ch, 1dc in first ch sp, *2ch, 1dc in next ch sp, 2ch, 1dc in next ch sp, 2ch, 1dc in next ch sp, 2ch, [1dc, 2ch, 1dc] in next ch sp; rep from * to end, ss in third of 5-ch, ss in fourth of same 5-ch.
**Round 6**: 5ch, 1dc in first ch sp, *2ch, 1dc in next ch sp, 2ch, 1dc in next ch sp, 2ch, 1dc in next ch sp, 2ch, 1dc in next ch sp, 2ch, [1dc, 2ch, 1dc] in next ch sp; rep from * to end, ss in third of 5-ch, ss in fourth of same 5-ch.
**Rounds 7–16**: 5ch, 1dc, 1ch in each ch sp around (36 sts), ss in third of 5-ch, ss in fourth of same 5-ch.
**Round 17**: 1ch, *2sc in next ch sp, 1sc in next ch sp, 3ch, ss in first ch, 1sc in same ch sp,

2sc in next ch sp, 3ch, ss in first ch; rep from * to end, ss in first ch to join round.
Fasten off.

## Flowers

Using B, make 4ch, ss in first ch to make a ring.
**Round 1**: [3ch, 1sc into middle of 4-ch] 5 times (5 holes for petals), ss in first ch.
**Round 2**: [1sc, 1hdc, 2dc, 1hdc, 1sc] in each ch sp, ss into base of first 3-ch from previous round.
Change to C.
**Round 3**: [Place the hook through center hole from front to back and back through middle hole of any petal, make 1sc, 3ch] 5 times.
**Round 4**: [1sc, 1dc, 1sc] in each ch sp, ss into base of first sc.
Fasten off.

## Finishing

Sew in ends. Weave ribbon around holes in stitches. Sew ends of ribbon together to attach.
Stitch flower to hat.

# Beanie Hat

A really simple beanie hat pattern decorated with a pretty boat motif. Always use a very soft yarn if making something that will be worn on a baby's head.

## Hat

Using A and D/3 (3mm) hook, make 4ch, ss in first ch to make a ring.

**Round 1**: 2ch, make 8hdc into ring, join with ss in first 2-ch. (8 sts)

**Round 2**: 2ch, 1hdc in same st, 2hdc in each st to end, join with ss in first 2-ch. (16 sts)

**Round 3**: 2ch, 1hdc in same st, *1hdc in next st, 2hdc in next st; rep from * to end, join with ss in first 2-ch. (24 sts)

**Round 4**: Rep Round 3. (36 sts)

**Round 5**: 2ch, 1hdc in same st, *1hdc in each of next 2 sts, 2hdc in next st; rep from * to last 2 sts, 1hdc in last 2 sts, join with ss in first 2-ch. (48 sts)

**Round 6**: 2ch, 1hdc in same st, *1hdc in each of next 7 sts, 2hdc in next st; rep from * to last 7 sts, 1hdc in each st to end, join with ss in first 2-ch. (54 sts)

**Round 7**: 2ch, 1hdc in same st, *1hdc in each of next 8 sts, 2hdc in next st; rep from * to last 8 sts, 1hdc in each st to end, join with ss in first 2-ch. (60 sts)

**Rounds 8–14**: 2ch, 1hdc in each st to end, join with ss in first 2-ch.

Join in B.

**Round 15**: 1sc in each st to end, join with ss.

Join in C.

**Round 16**: 1sc in each st to end, join with ss.

Fasten off.

## Boat motif base

Using red and C/2 (2.5mm) hook, make 9ch, 1sc in next ch from hook, 1hdc in next st, 1dc in next st, 1tr in next st, 1dc in next st, 1hdc in next st, 1sc, ss in first ch.

Fasten off.

## Boat motif sails

Using white and C/2 (2.5mm) hook, make 11ch, make 1sc in second ch from hook, 1sc in next ch, 1hdc in next ch, 1dc in each of next 2ch, 1tr in next ch, 1dtr in next ch, 1trtr in next ch.

Fasten off.

Working on other side of ch just worked with WS facing, join blue in underside of second sc, 1sc in next ch, 1hdc in next ch, 1dc in next ch, 1tr in next ch, 1dtr in next ch 1trtr in next ch, 6ch, join with ss in next ch.

Fasten off.

## Finishing

Sew boat motif sail onto boat base using yarn needle and attaching to the center bottom chain of the straighter edge of the bottom of boat.

Sew boat motif onto hat.

---

### Materials

**50% baby alpaca/50% merino light worsted (DK) yarn, such as Rooster Almerino Baby**

→ 1 x 1¾oz (50g) ball—approx. 136yds (125m)—each of off-white (A), green (B), and pale blue (C)

→ Scraps of red, white, and blue

→ D/3 (3mm) and C/2 (2.5mm) crochet hooks

### Abbreviations

**ch** chain; **dc** double crochet; **dtr** double treble; **hdc** half double crochet; **rep** repeat; **sc** single crochet; **sp** space; **ss** slip stitch; **st(s)** stitch(es); **tr** treble; **trtr** triple treble

### Size

**To fit age**: 3–6 months

### Finished size

**Circumference**: 14in. (35cm)

### Gauge

18 sts x 13 rows over a 4in. (10cm) square working in half double crochet using a D/3 (3mm) hook.

# Brimmed Baby Hat

A very pretty and cute hat for a toddler. This is made in a fine wool/silk yarn, which is very soft and easy to wear. Perfect for both keeping the sun off baby's head or keeping nice and warm in the winter.

## Hat

Using C/2 (2.5mm) hook and A, make 5ch, join with ss into first ch to make a ring.

**Round 1**: 12dc into ring.

**Round 2**: *1sc into first dc, 2sc into second dc; rep from * to end. (18 sts)

**Round 3**: *1sc in first st, 2sc in next st; rep from * to end. (24 sts)

Cont increasing in this way, making 2sc in first of 2 sts below and having one more stitch between increases, until work measures 3in. (7.5cm) from center of crown to edge.

**Next round**: 1sc in each st. (114 sts)

**Next round**: 1ch, *sc2tog, 1ch; rep from * to end. (115 sts)

**Next round**: *Sc2tog (draw yarn through st at each side of group below), 1ch; rep from * to end (114 sts)

Rep last round seven more times.

**Next round**: 1sc in each st.

**Make brim:**

**Round 32**: *1sc in each of next 5 sts, 2sc in next st; rep from * to end. (133 sts)

**Rounds 33–36**: 1sc in each st.

**Round 37**: As Round 32. (155 sts)

**Rounds 38–40**: 1sc in each st.

**Round 41**: *1sc in each of next 7 sts, 2sc in next st; rep from * to end. (173 sts)

**Rounds 42–43**: 1sc in each st.

Fasten off.

## Flowers (make 3)

Using A and F/5 (4mm) hook, make 6ch, join with ss into first chain to make a ring.

Make 16sc into ring, join with ss.

Fasten off.

Join B into fastened off st.

*3ch, 1dc into next 2 sts, 3ch, ss into next st; rep from * four times (5 petals).

Fasten off.

## Finishing

Sew in ends on hat.

Using a yarn needle weave around the center hole of flower to close and tighten; sew in ends.

Position flowers as required and stitch to hat.

### Materials

**55% merino/45% silk mix sportweight (4-ply) yarn, such as Fyberspates Scrumptious 4-ply**

➜ 1 x 3½oz (100g) skein—approx. 399yds. (365m) of gray (A)

**50% baby alpaca/50% merino mix light worsted (DK) yarn, such as Rooster Almerino DK**

➜ Small amount of bright pink (B)

➜ C/2 (2.5mm) and F/5 (4mm) crochet hooks

### Abbreviations

**ch** chain; **cont** continue; **dc** double crochet; **rep** repeat; **sc** single crochet; **sc2tog** (single crochet 2 together decrease) insert hook in next st, yo, pull yarn through (2 loops on hook). Without finishing st, insert hook in next st, yo, pull yarn through (3 loops on hook), yo, pull yarn through all 3 loops on hook; **ss** slip stitch; **st(s)** stitch(es); **yo** yarn over hook

### Size

**To fit age:** 12–36 months

### Finished size

**Circumference:** approx. 17–18in. (42.5–45cm)

# Ophelia Buggy Blanket

Just large enough to tuck in the toes, this is the perfect size for a buggy or car seat blanket. The color combinations are light and bright, which make it a suitable blanket for either a boy or a girl.

## Blanket

Change color on each row.

Using first color, make 83ch.

**Row 1:** 1dc in 2nd ch from hook, 1dc in next ch, *1dc in each of next 3 ch, dc3tog over next 3ch, 1dc in next 3-ch, 3dc in next ch; rep from * ending last rep with 2dc in last ch, turn.

**Row 2:** 3ch, 1dc in first st, *1dc in each of next 3 sts, dc3tog over next 3 sts, 1dc in each of next 3 sts, 3dc in next st; rep from * ending last rep with 2dc in top of turning chain, turn.

Change color.

Rep Row 2 another 48 times more, making a total of 50 rows.

Fasten off.

## Edging

**Round 1:** With RS facing, join A in fasten off st.

## Materials

**50% baby alpaca/50% merino mix light worsted (DK) yarn, such as Rooster Almerino DK**

→ 1 x 1¾oz (50g) ball—approx. 124yds (112.5m)—each of off-white (A), blue-green (B), bright pink (C), pale blue, pale pink, green, yellow, orange, dark purple, purple, and lilac

→ G/6 (4.5mm) crochet hook

## Abbreviations

**ch** chain; **dc** double crochet; **hdc** half double crochet; **rep** repeat; **RS** right side; **sc** single crochet; **ss** slip stitch; **st(s)** stitch(es); **yo** yarn over hook

## Special abbreviation

**dc3tog** (double crochet 3 together decrease) *yo, insert hook in next st, yo, pull yarn through, yo, pull yarn through 2 loops on hook (2 loops on hook). Without finishing st, rep from * in each of next 2 sts (4 loops on hook), yo, pull yarn through all 4 loops on hook

## Finished size

Approx. 20 x 25in. (50 x 62.5cm)

## Gauge

15 sts x 8 rows over a 4in. (10cm) square working double crochet using a G/6 (4.5mm) hook.

### Side 1 (Top):

1ch, 1sc in each of next 2 sts, 1hdc in each of next 2 sts, 1dc in each of next 3 sts, 1hdc in each of next 2 sts, *1sc in next 3 sts, 1hdc in each of next 2 sts, 1dc in each of next 3 sts, 1hdc in each of next 2 sts; rep from * to last 2 sts, 1sc in next st, 4sc in corner st.

### Side 2:

*Make 2sc in each color down side, 4sc in corner st.

### Side 3:

Working on bottom chain of Row 1 of blanket, 1dc in each of next 2 sts, 1hdc in each of next 2 sts; rep from * from Side 1 to last 6 sts, 1sc in each of next 3 sts, 1hdc in each of next 2 sts, 1dc in next st, 4sc in corner st.

### Side 4:

Rep Side 2 to last st, make 4sc in corner st, ss in first ch from Side 1.

Fasten off.

**Round 2**: Using B, make 1sc in each st around blanket, making 4sc in each corner st, join with a ss in first st.

**Round 3**: Rep Round 2.

Fasten off.

### Pompoms (make 4)

Using C, wrap the yarn around three or four fingers approx. 80 times. Gently slide the yarn off your fingers and tie a knot in the center very securely. The pompom will now have loops on either side of the knot. Cut all the loops; trim and fluff the pompom into shape.

### Finishing

Sew in ends.

Sew one pompom onto each corner of the blanket.

# Baby Mittens

A delicious mix of supersoft merino wool and silk—perfect to keep little fingers warm—these mittens are made using a traditional shell pattern with a little shell edging and tied with a pretty ribbon. They look very special but this is a really quick and easy pattern.

### Abbreviations

**ch** chain; **dc** double crochet; **hdc** half double crochet; **rep** repeat; **sp** space; **sc** single crochet; **ss** slip stitch; **st(s)** stitch(es)

### Size

**To fit age**: 0–6 months

### Finished size

**Length**: approx. 3½in. (9cm)

### Materials

**55% merino/45% silk mix sportweight (4-ply) yarn, such as Fyberspates Scrumptious 4-ply**

➜ 1 x 3½oz (100g) skein—approx. 399yds (365m)—of ecru or pink

➜ 40in. (1m) narrow blue or pink ribbon

➜ C/2 (2.5mm) crochet hook

## Mittens (make 2)

Make 4ch, ss in first ch to make a ring.

**Round 1**: 3ch (counts as 1dc), 11dc in ring, join with ss in top of first 3-ch. (12 sts)

**Round 2**: 3ch, 1dc in first st, 2dc in each st to end, join with ss in top of first 3-ch. (24 sts)

**Round 3**: 3ch, 4dc in same st as 3ch, *skip 1 st, 1sc in next st, skip 1 st, 5dc in next st; rep from * to end, join with ss in base of 3-ch from previous round.

**Round 4**: Ss in each of next 2 sts, 1ch, *5dc in next sc from previous round, 1sc in middle st of 5-dc shell, 5dc in next sc from previous round; rep from * to end, join with ss in top of first 1-ch.

**Round 5**: 3ch, 4dc in same st as 3-ch, *1sc in middle st of 5-dc shell, 5dc in next sc from previous round; rep from * to end, join with ss in top of first dc.

Insert st marker at beginning of next round.

**Round 6**: Rep Round 4.

**Round 7**: Rep Round 5.

**Round 8**: Rep Round 4.

**Round 9**: 2ch, * skip next 2 sts, 1hdc in next st; rep from * to end, join with ss in top of first 2-ch.

**Round 10**: 2ch, *2hdc in next sp, 1hdc in next sc, ss in top of first 2-ch.

**Round 11**: *1sc in next st, skip 1 st, 5dc in next st, skip 1 st; rep from * to end, join in first sc with ss.

## Finishing

Sew in ends.

Thread ribbon through spaces around top and tie a bow.

# Sweetheart Blanket

This is a a gorgeous crib blanket or sitting-on-the-couch-blanket.

All the squares are exactly the same heart design, but made in

a variety of pretty colors.

## Materials

**50% baby alpaca/50% merino mix light worsted (DK) yarn, such as Rooster Almerino DK**

→ 10 x 1¾oz (50g) balls— approx. 1240yds (1125m)—of off-white (MC)

→ 1 x 1¾oz (50g) ball—approx. 124yds (112.5m)—each of orange, yellow, light blue, pale pink, bright pink, purple, light green, lilac, and turquoise (CC)

→ D/3 (3mm) and F/5 (4mm) crochet hooks

## Abbreviations

**CC** contrast color; **ch** chain; **hdc** half double crochet; **MC** main color; **patt** pattern; **rep** repeat; **RS** right side; **sc** single crochet; **ss** slip stitch; **st(s)** stitch(es); **yo** yarn over hook

## Finished size

**Each square:** 4in. (10cm)

**Blanket:** 36 x 30½in. (92 x 76.5cm)

## Gauge

21 rows x 21 sts over a 4in. (10cm) square working single crochet using a D/3 (3mm) hook.

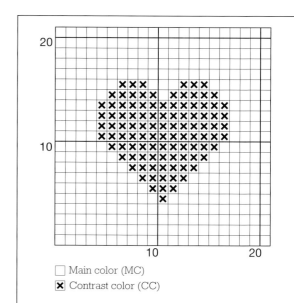

☐ Main color (MC)
☒ Contrast color (CC)

## Squares (make 63)

Using sc throughout, make 7 squares of each CC color heart on a background of MC, following chart.

## Finishing

Lay squares out on a flat surface in strips of 7 across by 9 down so different color hearts are arranged evenly across the blanket.

Using sc and A, join rows into strips. Join strips together vertically.

**Edging:**

**Round 1**: Join A in top right-hand corner of blanket, make 1sc into same corner, *1sc in each st along edge to next corner, 2sc in corner sts; rep from * twice more, 1sc in each st along edge to last corner, 1sc in corner st, ss into first sc.

**Round 2**: 1ch, 1sc in each st along edge to next corner, 2sc in corner sts; rep from * twice more, 1sc in each st along edge to next corner, ss into first 1-ch.

**Round 3**: 3ch, 1dc in each st along edge to next corner, 2dc in corner sts; rep from * twice more, 1dc in each st along edge to next corner, ending 1dc into same space as first 3-ch, ss into top of first 3-ch.

Fasten off.

## Materials

**50% baby alpaca/50% merino mix light worsted (DK) yarn, such as Rooster Almerino DK**

→ 1 x 1¾oz (50g) ball—approx. 124yds (112.5m)—each of green (A) and off-white (B)

→ E/4 (3.5mm) crochet hook

## Abbreviations

**ch** chain; **hdc** half double crochet; **rep** repeat; **sc** single crochet; **ss** slip stitch; **st(s)** stitch(es); **yo** yarn over hook

## Special abbreviations

**Cl** (Cluster) yo, insert hook in st, yo, pull yarn through, yo, insert hook in same st, yo, pull yarn through, yo, insert hook in same st, yo, pull yarn through, yo (7 loops on hook), pull yarn through all 7 loops on hook, yo, 1ch (1 cluster made)

**hdc2tog** (half double crochet 2 together decrease) *yo, insert hook in next st, yo, pull yarn through (3 loops on hook). Without finishing st, rep from * in next st (5 loops on hook), yo, pull yarn through all 5 loops on hook

## Size

**To fit age**: approx. 12–36 months

## Finished size

**Length from crown to edge**: 7in. (17.5cm)
**Circumference** 18–20in. (45–50cm)

# Pompom Hat

This very cute hat is made with super soft alpaca and merino mix so it will not irritate delicate skin. It's such an easy hat to crochet that it can be made over one evening.

## Hat

Using A, make 76ch.

**Row 1**: 1sc in next ch from hook, 1sc in each ch to end.

**Rows 2–3**: 1ch, 1sc in each st to end.

**Row 4**: 1ch, 1sc in each of next 5 sts, 2sc in next st, *1sc in each of next 4 sts, 2sc in next st; rep from * to last 5 sts, 1sc in each of next 5 sts. (90 sts)

**Row 5**: 1sc in each st to end. (90 sts)
    Change to B.

**Rows 6–7**: 1sc in each st. (90 sts)
    Change to A.

**Rows 8–9**: 1sc in each st. (90 sts)
    Change to B.

**Row 10**: 3ch, *1Cl in next st, skip 1 st; rep from * to last st, 1hdc.
    Change to A.

**Rows 11–12**: 2ch, 1hdc in each st to end.

**Row 13**: 2ch, *1hdc in each of next 7 sts, hdc2tog; rep from * to end. (80 sts)
    Change to B.

**Row 14**: 3ch, skip first st, *1Cl in next st, skip 1 st; rep from * to last st, 1hdc.
    Change to A.

**Row 15**: 1ch, 1sc in each st to end.

**Row 16**: 2ch, *1hdc in each of next 6 sts, hdc2tog; rep from * to end. (70 sts)

**Row 17**: 2ch, *1hdc in each st to end.

**Row 18**: 2ch, *1hdc in each of next 5 sts, hdc2tog; rep from * to end. (60 sts)

**Row 19**: 2ch, *1hdc in each st to end.

**Row 20**: 2ch, *1hdc in each of next 4 sts, hdc2tog; rep from * to end. (50 sts)

**Row 21**: Rep Row 19.

**Row 22**: 2ch, hdc2tog, *1hdc in each of next 3 sts, hdc2tog; rep from * to end. (40 sts)

**Row 23**: 2ch, *1hdc in each of next 2 sts, hdc2tog; rep from * to end. (30 sts)

**Row 24**: 2ch, *hdc2tog, 1hdc in next st; rep from * to end. (20 sts)
    Fasten off leaving a long tail approx. 12in. (30cm).

## Finishing

Sew in ends.

    Make a running stitch around last row. Pull yarn tight and gather top together, then sew in securely.

    Oversew seam together.

    Using A and B together, wrap the yarn around two or three fingers approx. 80 times. Gently slide the yarn off your fingers and tie a knot in the center very securely. The pompom will now have loops on either side of the knot. Cut all the loops; trim and fluff the pompom into shape and sew onto top of hat.

# Flower Bonnet

This little bonnet has a really vintage look with different pinks, purples, and yellow flowers sewn onto a basic bonnet shape and tied with a pretty ribbon under the chin. It's a lovely warm, cozy hat for those chilly days walking in the park.

## EXPERT ADVICE

*Make enough flowers to fit all around the hat and completely cover the surface of the base bonnet. Always sew in ends and weave in and out of stitches at back of centers to close the holes.*

## Materials

**50% baby alpaca/50% merino light worsted (DK) yarn, such as Rooster Almerino Baby**

→ 1 x 1¾oz (50g) ball—approx. 136yds (125m)—of off-white (A)
→ Scraps of yellow, off-white, light pink, dark pink, purple, green, and lilac
→ D/3 (3mm) crochet hook
→ 40in. (1m) of ⅝in. (1.5cm) wide ribbon

## Abbreviations

**ch** chain; **dc** double crochet; **dtr** double treble; **hdc** half double crochet; **rep** repeat; **sc** single crochet; **sp** space; **ss** slip stitch; **st(s)** stitch(es); **tr** treble;

## Size

**To fit age**: 0–6 months

## Finished size

**Circumference**: approx. 15in. (37.5cm)

## Gauge

15 sts x 8 rows over a 4in. (10cm) square working double crochet using a D/3 (3mm) hook.

## Bonnet

Using A, make 4ch, ss in first ch to form a ring.

**Round 1**: 2ch (counts as 1hdc), 15hdc in ring, join with ss in top of first 2-ch. (16 sts)

**Round 2**: 3ch, 1dc in next st, 2dc in next and each st to end, join with a ss in top of first 3-ch. (32 sts)

**Round 3**: 3ch, 1dc in base of first 3-ch, *1dc in each of next 2 sts, 2dc in next st; rep from * around, join with ss in top of first 3-ch. (42 sts)

**Round 4**: 3ch, 1dc in base of first 3-ch, *1dc in each of next 3 sts, 2dc in next st; rep from * around, join with ss in top of first 3-ch. (52 sts)

**Round 5**: 3ch, 1dc in base of first 3-ch, 1dc in each st around, join with ss in top of first 3-ch. (52 sts)

**Round 6**: 1ch, 1sc in between each dc to end, join with ss in top of first 1-ch. (52 sts)

Rep Rounds 5 and 6 three times more.

**Round 13**: Rep Round 5.

**Round 14**: 1ch, *skip 1 st, 1sc in next st, skip 1 st, 5dc in next st (1 shell); rep from * until 8 shells are made ending 1sc, 1ss in next st.

Fasten off.

## Lazy daisy (make approx. 7)

Using first color, make 6ch, ss in first ch to form a ring.

**Round 1**: 1ch, 11sc in ring, join in next color, ss to join in first 1-ch. (12 sts)

**Petals:**
Continue with second color.

**Round 2**: [9ch, ss in next st] 12 times, ending with ss in ss of first round.

Weave around center to close center hole.
Fasten off.

## Apple blossom (make approx. 4)

Using first color, make 4ch, ss in first ch to form a ring.

**Round 1**: 2ch, 9sc in ring, using second color, ss in top of first 2-ch.

Continue with second color.

**Round 2**: 1ch *[1tr, 2dtr, 1tr] in next st, ss in next st; rep from * 3 times more. [1tr, 2dtr, 1tr] in next st, ss in first 1-ch. (5 petals)

Fasten off.

## Petal blossom (make approx. 10)

Using any color, make 6ch, ss in first ch to form a ring.

16sc in ring, join with ss, *3ch, 1dc in each of next 2 sts, 3ch, ss in next st; rep from * 4 more times. (5 petals)

Weave around center to close center hole.
Fasten off.

## Remember me blossom (make approx. 5)

Using first color, make 4ch, ss in first ch to form a ring.

**Round 1**: 2ch, 9sc in ring, using second color, ss in top of first 2-ch. (10 sts)

Continue with second color.

**Round 2**: 5ch, 1dtr in each of next 9 sts, ss in top of first 5-ch.

Fasten off.
Turn petals inside out.

## Cherry blossom (make approx. 5)

Using any color, make 4ch, ss in first ch to form a ring.

*3ch, 1dc in ring, 3ch, ss in ring; rep from * until 5 petals are made.

Fasten off.

## Finishing

Use a yarn needle to weave loose ends around center of flowers to close center hole. Stitch flowers to bonnet. Sew in ends.

Cut ribbon in half and attach each end approx. ½in. (1cm) down from last shell edge.

# Star Stitch Bootees

Use a pretty toggle to embellish these cute little bootees, which match the Toggle Jacket on page 92. The star stitch is simple once you get the idea and these would make a perfect gift.

## Materials

**50% baby alpaca/50% merino light worsted (DK) yarn, such as Rooster Almerino Baby**
→ 1 x 1¾oz (50g) ball—approx. 136yds (125m)—of green
→ D/3 (3mm) crochet hook
→ 2 small toggle buttons

## Abbreviations

**ch** chain; **hdc** half double crochet; **patt** pattern; **rep** repeat; **RS** right side; **sc** single crochet; **ss** slip stitch; **st(s)** stitch(es); **yo** yarn over hook

## Special abbreviations

**SS1** (Star Stitch 1) 3ch, insert hook in second ch from hook, yo, pull yarn through (2 loops on hook), insert hook in next ch, yo, pull yarn through (3 loops on hook), insert hook in base of ch, yo, pull yarn through (4 loops on hook), insert hook in each of next 2 sts bringing a loop through each time (6 loops on the hook) yo, pull yarn through all 6 loops, 1ch

**SS2** (Star Stitch 2) insert hook through 1-ch of SS just made, pull yarn through (2 loops), insert hook through front of last loop of previous SS, pull yarn through, insert hook through base st of last loop of

## Base (make 2)

Make 14ch.

**Round 1**: 2sc in second ch from hook, 1sc in each of next 5ch, 1hdc in each of next 5ch, 2hdc in next ch, 3hdc in last ch. (17 sts)

Working on other side of chain, 2hdc in next ch, 1hdc in each of next 5ch, 1sc in each of next 5 sts, 2sc in last ch, join with ss in top of first sc. (31 sts)

**Round 2**: 3ch, 2dc in base of ss, 1dc in next st, 2dc in next st. 1dc in each of next 9 sts, *3dc in next st, 1dc in next st; rep from * three times more, 1dc in each of next 9 sts, 2dc in next st, join with ss in top of first 3-ch. (41 sts)

**Round 3**: 3ch, 1dc in base of ss, 1dc in each of next 20 sts, 2dc in next st, 1dc in next st, 2dc in next st, 1dc in each of next 17 sts, 2dc in

previous SS, pull yarn through, *insert hook through next st and pull loop through; rep from * once more (6 loops on hook), yo, pull yarn through all 6 loops, 1ch.

## Size

**To fit age**: 0–6 months

## Finished size

**Length**: approx. 3½in. (9cm)

next st, join with ss in top of first 3-ch. (46 sts)

**Begin working star st patt in rows:**

**Row 1**: [SS1 (once only), SS2] to end of row, join with ss in first 3-ch, turn.

**Row 2**: 2ch, 2hdc in center of each star stitch to end of row, join with ss in top of first 3-ch. (46 sts)

Fasten off.

**Top (make 1 left and 1 right)**

Make 40ch.

**Row 1**: SS1 to end of row.

**Row 2**: 2ch, 2hdc in center of each star stitch to end of row, join with ss in top of first 3-ch.

**Row 3**: SS1 once, SS2 to end of row, join with a ss in first 2-ch.

**Row 4**: As Row 2.(For left foot shaping only, fasten off and see instruction below for left foot shaping).

**Shaping for right foot:**

**Row 1**: SS1 once, [SS2] four times, 1hdc in top of 2-ch from previous row, turn.

**Row 2**: 2ch, 1hdc in center of first star stitch, *2hdc in center of each of next 2 star stitches, 1hdc in last star stitch, 1sc in top of first star stitch from previous row, turn.

**Row 3**: SS1 once, [SS2] three times, 1hdc in top of 2-ch from previous row, turn.

**Row 4**: 2ch, 1hdc in center of first star stitch, 2hdc in next star stitch, 1hdc into last star stitch, 1sc in top of star stitch from previous row, turn.

**Row 5**: SS1 once, SS2 once, 1hdc in top of 2-ch from previous row, turn.

Fasten off.

**Shaping for left foot:**

Count 11 sts from left-hand side of work and join yarn in eleventh stitch. Repeat Rows 1–5 as for right foot shaping.

Fasten off.

**Finishing**

With RS facing, match center top with center base and pin. To create flap for toggle, start sewing from two star stitches down and then sew top around bootee.

Sew toggle button onto side back.

**Toggle loop:**

Pick up 1 st at front side corresponding with toggle, make 8ch, join with a ss in first ch.

Fasten off.

Sew in ends.

# Flower Crib Blanket

A warm, cozy blanket, big enough for a crib. This is made up of squares, so a great project and easy to make one or two squares per evening before the baby is born.

**Materials**

**50% baby alpaca/50% merino wool mix worsted (Aran) yarn, such as Rooster Almerino Aran**

➔ 10 x 1¾oz (50g) balls—approx. 1030yds (940m)—of off-white (A)

➔ 6 x 1¾oz (50g) balls—approx. 618yds (564m)—of pale pink (B)

➔ G/6 (4.5mm) and H/8 (5mm) crochet hook

**Abbreviations**

**beg** beginning; **ch** chain; **hdc** half double crochet; **patt** pattern; **rep** repeat; **sc** single crochet; **sp(s)** space(es); **ss** slip stitch; **st(s)** stitch(es); **yo** yarn over hook

**Finished size**

Approx. 28 x 38in. (70 x 95cm)

**Gauge**

Each square measures approx. 5 x 5in. (12.5 x 12.5cm).

**Flower square (make 35)**

Using A and G/6 (4.5mm) hook, make 8ch, join with ss in first ch to make a ring.

**Round 1**: 1ch, 18sc into ring, ss in first sc. (18 sts)

**Round 2**: 1ch, *3ch, skip 2 sts, 1sc in next st; rep from * 5 times more, ss in first of 3-ch. (6 loops)

**Round 3**: 1ch, [1sc, 3ch, 5dc, 3ch, 1sc] into each of next 6 ch sps, ss in first 1-ch. (6 petals)

**Round 4**: 1ch, [1sc between 2-sc from previous round (between two petals), 5ch behind petal of previous round] 6 times, ss in first ch. (6 petals)

**Round 5**: 1ch, [1sc, 3ch, 7dc, 3ch, 1sc] in each of next 6 5-ch sps, ss in first ch.

Fasten off.

**Round 6**: Join B between 2-sc of previous round (between any two petals), 1ch, 1sc into same sp, [6ch (working behind petals) 1sc between next 2-sc of previous round] 6 times, ss in first ch.

**Round 7**: Ss in next sp, 3ch (counts as 1dc), *[4dc, 2ch, 2dc] into same sp, 6dc in next sp, [2dc, 2ch, 4dc] in next sp**, 1dc in next sp; rep from * to ** once more, ss in top of first 3-ch.

**Round 8**: 3ch (counts as 1dc), 1dc in each of next 4-dc from previous round, *[3dc, 2ch, 3dc] in next 2-ch sp, 1dc in each of next 9-dc; rep from * to last 4dc, 1dc in each of last 4-dc, join with a ss into top of first 3-ch.

**Round 9**: 3ch, *1dc in each st to next corner sp, [3dc, 2ch, 3dc] into corner sp; rep from * to end, ss into top of first 3-ch.

Fasten off.

**Finishing**

Sew in ends. Arrange squares 7 down by 5 across.

Using A, work sc seam to join squares.

**Edging:**

With RS facing and using H/8 (5mm) hook, join A in any corner ch sp.

**Round 1**: 1ch, 1sc in same ch sp (first corner), *1sc in each st along each square to next corner, (do not make a sc into the seams, but make 1sc each side of each seam), 2sc in corner ch sp; rep from * twice more, 1sc in each st to last corner, join with ss in first 1-ch.

**Round 2**: 3ch, 2dc in same sp as 3-ch (first corner), *1dc in each st to next corner, 3dc in corner st; rep from * twice more, 1dc in each st to last corner, join with ss in top of first 3-ch. Break off A.

**Round 3**: Join in B, *1sc in next st, skip next st, 5dc in next st, skip next st; rep from * to end, join with ss into joining st.

Fasten off.

# CHAPTER THREE

# Jackets, Shawls, and Dresses

# Hooded Jacket

A very cool and trendy jacket. It's embellished with a double row of big colorful buttons at the front and a bright orange pompom at the point on the hood. So cute, everyone in the family will want one!

## Materials

**50% baby alpaca/50% merino wool mix worsted (Aran) yarn, such as Rooster Almerino Aran**

→ 5:5:6:6:7:7 x 1¾oz (50g) balls—approx. 515:**515**:618:**618**:721:**721**yds (470:**470**:564:**564**:658:**658**m)—of pale gray (A)

→ 1 x 1¾oz (50g) ball—approx. 103yds (94m)—of orange (B)

→ F/5 (4mm) crochet hook

→ 6 x 1in. (2.5cm) diameter 4-hole buttons in a variety of colors

## Abbreviations

**ch** chain; **cont** continue; **patt** pattern(s); **rep** repeat; **RS** right side; **sc** single crochet; **ss** slip stitch; **st(s)** stitch(es); **WS** wrong side

## Special abbreviation

**V-st** 1sc, 1ch, 1sc in next st

## Size

**To fit age**: 0–3:**3–6**:6–12:**12–18**:18–24:**24–36** months

## Finished size

| Chest | (in.): | 19¼ | 21½ | 24 | 27 | 29 | 32 |
|---|---|---|---|---|---|---|---|
| | (cm): | 48 | 54 | 60 | 67.5 | 72 | 80 |
| Length | (in.): | 9 | 10½ | 12¼ | 14 | 15½ | 17 |
| | (cm): | 22.5 | 26.5 | 31 | 35 | 39 | 42 |
| Sleeve seam | (in.): | 5 | 6¼ | 7¾ | 10¼ | 11 | 12 |
| | (cm): | 12.5 | 15.5 | 19.5 | 26 | 27.5 | 30 |

## Gauge

8 patt x 18 rows over a 4in. (10cm) square using a F/5 (4mm) hook.

## Body

Using A, make 102:**114**:126:**138**:150:**162**ch.

**Row 1:** 1sc in second ch from hook, skip 1 ch, *1V-st in next ch, skip 2 ch; rep from * to end, ending last rep skip 1 ch, 1sc in last ch, turn. (101:**113**:125:**137**:149:**161** sts)

**Row 2 (patt row):** 1ch, 1sc in first sc, skip 2 sts, *make 1V-st in next st, skip 2 sts; rep from * to end, ending last rep skip 1 sc, 1sc in last st.

Rep Row 2 until body measures 4¾:**5¼**:6:**7**:7½:**8½**in.(12:**13**:15:**17.5**:19:**21**cm) ending with a RS row.

### First buttonhole:

**Next row:** With WS facing, 1ch, 1sc in first sc, 3ch, skip 1 V-st group, *1V-st in next ch sp; rep from * ending skip 1 sc, 1sc in last st. (101:**113**:125:**137**:149:**161** sts, 33:**37**:41:**45**:49:**53** patts)

**Next row:** Patt to buttonhole space, 1V-st in buttonhole sp, patt to end.

Work 6 rows in patt.

### Divide for armholes:

Work 7:**8**:9:**10**:11:**12** patt, skip 1 sc, 1sc in next sc, turn.

Working on following 23:**26**:29:**32**:35:**38** sts only, work 7:**8**:9:**10**:11:**12** patt for left front.

Work 4 rows in patt.

**Next two rows:** Rep two buttonhole rows as before.

Cont working straight for 10 rows.

**Next two rows:** Rep two buttonhole rows as before.

Cont working straight until armhole measures 4¾:**4¾**:5:**5½**:6:**7**in. (12:**12**:12.5:**14**:15:**17.5**cm) ending with a WS row.

Work 1 more row in patt.

Fasten off.

**Shoulder:**

Place a marker 9:**11**:13:**15**:17:**19** sts in from armhole edge to mark inner edge of shoulder seam leaving 14:**15**:16:**17**:18:**19** sts unworked at front opening edge.

**Shape back:**

With WS facing, return to last complete row worked, skip next 10 sts, join yarn in next sc, 1ch, 1sc in joining st, skip 1 sc, 1V-st in next ch sp, patt until 11:**13**:15:**17**:19:**21** patt in total have been worked, skip 1 sc, 1sc in next sc, turn.

Work on these 35:**41**:47:**53**:59:**65** sts, 11:**13**:15:**17**:19:**21** patt (back) until work measures 4¼:**5**:5½:**6**:6½:**7**in. (10.5:**12.5**:14:**15**:16.5:**17.5**cm) ending with a RS row.

Fasten off.

**Shoulder:**

Place marker either side of center 17:**19**:21:**23**:25:**27** sts for back neck.

**Shape right front:**

With WS facing, return to last complete row worked, skip next 10 sts, join yarn in next sc, 1ch, 1sc in joining st, 1ch, skip 1 sc, 1V-st in next ch sp, patt to end, turn. (23:**26**:29:**32**:35:**38** sts, 7:**8**:9:**10**:11:**12** patt)

Finish to match left front.

Do not fasten off at end of right front, place loop onto safety pin (to be used later for hood).

**Sleeves (make 2)**

Make 24:**27**:27:**30**:30:**33**ch.

Rep Rows 1 and 2 as for Body. (23:**26**:26:**29**:29:**32** sts, 7:**8**:8:**9**:9:**10** patt)

**Row 3:** 1ch, 2sc in first sc, skip 1 sc, 1V-st in next ch sp, patt until V-st has been worked in last ch sp, skip 1 sc, 2sc in first sc, turn.

**Row 4:** 1ch, 2sc in first sc, 1sc in next sc, skip 1 sc, 1 V-st in next ch sp, patt until V-st has been worked in last ch sp, skip 1 sc, 1sc in next sc, 2sc in last sc, turn.

**Row 5:** 1ch, 1sc in first sc, 1V-st in next ch sp, skip 2 sc, 1V-st in next ch sp, patt until V-st has been worked in last ch sp, skip 2 sc, 1V-st in next ch sp, 1sc in last sc, turn. (29:**32**:32:**35**:35:**37** sts, 9:**10**:10:**11**:11:**12** patt)

Work 1:**3**:3:**5**:5:**6** rows in patt.

Rep last 4:**6**:6:**8**:8:**9** rows 1:**1**:2:**2**:3:**4** times more, then Rows 3–5 once again. (41:**44**:50:**53**:56:**62** sts, 13:**14**:16:**17**:18:**20** patt)

Work straight in patt until sleeve measures 5:**6¼**:7¾:**10¼**:11:**12**in. (12.5:**15.5**:19.5:**26**:27.5:**30**cm).

**Shape top:**

Place markers at each end of last row to mark top of sleeve seam.

Work a further 3 rows.

Fasten off.

**Finishing**

Join shoulder seams.

**Hood:**

Pick up loop left on safety pin at end of right front. Work across sts of right front neck, back neck, left front neck as follows:

1ch, 1sc in first sc, skip 1 sc, 1V-st in next ch sp, skip 2 sc, 1V-st in next ch sp, [skip 1 st, 1V-st in next st] 8:**9**:10:**11**:12:**13** times, 1V-st in next ch sp (center back neck ch sp), [1V-st in next st, skip 1 st] 8:**9**:10:**11**:12:**13** times, 1V-st in next ch sp, skip 2 sc, 1V-st in next ch sp, skip 1 sc, 1sc in last sc, turn. (65:**71**:77:**83**:89:**95** sts, 21:**23**:25:**27**:29:**31** patt)

Work in patt until hood measures 7:**7½**:8¼:**8½**:9:**10**in. (17.5:**19**:20.5:**22**:21.5:**25**cm).

Fold hood in half with RS together and join using overstitch with yarn sewing needle.

Fasten off.

Join sleeve seams below markers. Match sleeve markers to center of sts skipped at underarm and center of last row of sleeve to shoulder seam, sew sleeves into armholes.

Using B, make a small pompom and sew onto tip of hood.

**Buttonband and edging**

With RS facing skip corner st at right front bottom edge and join yarn in next st up side.

**Row 1**: Sc evenly along right front, hood, left front, bottom edge, making 3sc in corner st of bottom left front, ending 3sc in corner st at bottom right front. Join with ss in first sc.

**Row 2**: 1ch, 1sc in each st up right front edge finishing at start of hood, turn.

**Rows 3–4**: 1ch, 1sc in each st to end.

**Row 5**: 1ch, 1sc in each st to end, make 2sc in next st around corner. Join with ss in first 3-sc from Row 1.

Fasten off.

# *Poncho*

Ponchos are ideal for slipping on for extra warmth on chilly spring or autumn days. This toddler poncho is made using simple clusters and embellished with a pretty flower.

### Materials

**50% baby alpaca/50% merino mix light worsted (DK) yarn, such as Rooster Almerino DK**

➜ 4 x 1¾oz (50g) balls—approx. 496yds (450m)—of bright pink (A)
➜ Small amounts of off-white (B) and pale green (C)
➜ F/5 (4mm) crochet hook

### Abbreviations

**ch** chain; **ch sp** chain space; **hdc** half double crochet; **patt** pattern; **rep** repeat; **sc** single crochet; **sp** space; **ss** slip stitch; **st(s)** stitch(es); **WS** wrong side; **yo** yarn over hook

### Special abbreviations

**Cl** (Cluster) yo, insert hook in st, yo, pull yarn through, yo, insert hook in same st, yo, pull yarn through, yo, insert hook in same st, yo, pull yarn through, yo (7 loops on hook), pull yarn through all 7 loops on hook, yo, 1ch
**make corner** 1Cl, 3ch, 1Cl

### Size

**To fit age**: 6–18 months

### Finished size

**Circumference**: 20in. (50cm)
**Length**: 12in. (30cm)

### Gauge

8 clusters x 6½ rows over a 4in. (10cm) square using a F/5 (4mm) crochet hook.

## Poncho

Using A, make 76ch, join with ss in first ch, taking care not to twist chain.

**Round 1**: 1Cl, skip 1 ch, *1Cl, skip 1 ch; rep from * to end, ss to top of first Cl. (38 clusters)

**Round 2**: 1Cl in first ch sp, [1Cl in next ch sp] 17 times (18 clusters), make corner in next ch sp, 1Cl, 3ch, 1Cl, 18Cl in the last ch sp, make corner, 1Cl, 3ch, 1Cl, ss to top of first Cl. (36 clusters + 2 corners)

**Round 3**: 1Cl in sp below in same ss from end of previous row, [1Cl in each ch sp] 18 times (19 clusters), make corner in 3-ch sp, [1Cl in each following ch sp] 19 times, make corner in 3-ch sp, ss to top of first Cl. (38 clusters + 2 corners)

**Round 4**: 1Cl in sp below finishing ss, [1Cl in each ch sp] 19 times (20 clusters), make corner in 3-ch sp, [1Cl in each ch sp] 20 times, make corner in 3-ch sp, ss to top of first Cl. (40 clusters + 2 corners)

**Round 5**: 1Cl in sp below finishing ss, [1Cl in each ch sp] 20 times (21 clusters), make corner in 3-ch sp, [1Cl in each ch sp] 21 times, make corner in 3-ch sp, ss to top of first Cl. (42 clusters + 2 corners)

**Round 6**: 1Cl in sp below finishing ss, [1Cl in each ch sp] 21 times (22 clusters), make corner in 3-ch sp, [1Cl in each ch sp] 22 times, make corner in 3-ch sp, ss to top of first Cl. (44 clusters + 2 corners)

**Round 7**: 1Cl in sp below finishing ss, [1Cl in each ch sp] 22 times (23 clusters), make corner in 3-ch sp, [1Cl in each ch sp] 23 times, make corner in 3-ch sp, ss to top of first Cl. (46 clusters + 2 corners)

**Round 8**: 1Cl in sp below finishing ss, [1Cl in each ch sp] 23 times (24 clusters), make corner in 3-ch sp, [1Cl in each ch sp] 24 times, make corner in 3-ch sp, ss to top of first Cl. (48 clusters + 2 corners)

**Round 9**: 1Cl in sp below finishing ss, [1Cl in each ch sp] 24 times (25 clusters), make corner in 3-ch sp, [1Cl in each ch sp] 25 times, make corner in 3-ch sp, ss to top of first Cl. (50 clusters + 2 corners)

**Round 10**: 1Cl in sp below finishing ss, [1Cl in each ch sp] 25 times (26 clusters), make corner in 3-ch sp, [1Cl in each ch sp] 26 times, make corner in 3-ch sp, ss to top of first Cl. (52 clusters + 2 corners)

**Round 11**: 1Cl in sp below finishing ss, [1Cl in each ch sp] 26 times (27 clusters), make corner in 3-ch sp, [1Cl in each ch sp] 27 times, make corner in 3-ch sp, ss to top of first Cl. (54 clusters + 2 corners)

**Round 12**: 1Cl in sp below finishing ss, [1Cl in each ch sp] 27 times (28 clusters), make corner in 3-ch sp, [1Cl in each ch sp] 28 times, make corner in 3-ch sp, ss to top of first Cl. (56 clusters + 2 corners)

**Round 13**: 1Cl in sp below finishing ss, [1Cl in each ch sp] 28 times (29 clusters), make corner in 3-ch sp, [1Cl in each ch sp] 29 times, make corner in 3-ch sp, ss to top of first Cl. (58 clusters + 2 corners)

**Round 14**: 1Cl in sp below finishing ss, [1Cl in each ch sp] 29 times (30 clusters), make corner in 3-ch sp, [1Cl in each ch sp] 30 times, make corner in 3-ch sp, ss to top of first Cl. (60 clusters + 2 corners)

**Round 15**: 1Cl in sp below finishing ss, [1Cl in each ch sp] 30 times (31 clusters), make corner in 3-ch sp, [1Cl in each ch sp] 31 times, make corner in 3-ch sp, ss to top of first Cl. (62 clusters + 2 corners)

**Round 16**: 1Cl in sp below finishing ss, [1Cl in each ch sp] 31 times (32 clusters), make corner in 3-ch sp, [1Cl in each ch sp] 32 times, make corner in 3-ch sp, ss to top of first Cl. (64 clusters + 2 corners)

**Round 17**: 1Cl in sp below finishing ss, [1Cl in each ch sp] 32 times (33 clusters), make corner in 3-ch sp, [1Cl in each ch sp] 33 times, make corner in 3-ch sp, ss to top of first Cl. (66 clusters + 2 corners)

**Round 18**: 1Cl in sp below finishing ss, [1Cl in each ch sp] 33 times (34 clusters), make corner in 3-ch sp, [1Cl in each ch sp] 34 times, make corner in 3-ch sp, ss to top of first Cl. (68 clusters + 2 corners)

**Round 19**: 1Cl in sp below finishing ss, [1Cl in each ch sp] 34 times (35 clusters), make corner in 3-ch sp, [1Cl in each ch sp] 35 times, make corner in 3-ch sp, ss to top of first Cl. (70 clusters + 2 corners)

**Round 20**: 1Cl in sp below finishing ss, [1Cl in each ch sp] 35 times (36 clusters), make corner in 3-ch sp, [1Cl in each ch sp] 36 times, make corner in 3-ch sp, ss to top of first Cl. (72 clusters + 2 corners)

**Round 21**: 1Cl in sp below finishing ss, [1Cl in each ch sp] 36 times (37 clusters), make corner in 3-ch sp, [1Cl in each ch sp] 37 times, make corner in 3-ch sp, ss to top of first Cl. (74 clusters + 2 corners)

**Round 22**: 1Cl in sp below finishing ss, [1Cl in each ch sp] 37 times (38 clusters), make corner in 3-ch sp, [1Cl in each ch sp] 38 times, make corner in 3-ch sp, ss to top of first Cl. (76 clusters + 2 corners)

**Round 23**: 1Cl in sp below finishing ss, [1Cl in each ch sp] 38 times (39 clusters), make corner in 3-ch sp, [1Cl in each ch sp] 39 times, make corner in 3-ch sp, ss to top of first Cl. (78 clusters + 2 corners)

**Round 24**: 1Cl in sp below finishing ss, [1Cl in each ch sp] 39 times (40 clusters), make corner in 3-ch sp, [1Cl in each ch sp] 40 times, make corner in 3-ch sp, ss to top of first Cl. (80 clusters + 2 corners)

Do not fasten off.

**Bottom edging:**

1ch, 1sc in same space as chain (between 2-clusters of previous round), 1sc in each st and ch sp to end, ss to top of first sc.

Fasten off.

**Neck edging:**

Join yarn to ch at center back neck edge.

**Round 1**: 1sc in each st and ch sp to end, ss in first sc.

Rep Round 1 twice more.

Fasten off.

**Large flower**

Using B, make 5ch, join with a ss in first ch to make a ring.

**Round 1**: *1sc, 1dc, 1sc in ring; rep from * 3 times. (4 petals)

**Round 2**: *2ch, from WS ss in base of second sc of next petal (pick up 2 loops); rep from * 3 times more, slip last st in first ss. (4 loops)

**Round 3**: *4dc in next 2ch sp (at back), ss in same ch sp; rep from * 3 times more.

Fasten off.

Change to C, join yarn at base of highest point of previous round.

**Round 4**: *3ch, ss in middle of base of next petal (pick up 2 loops); rep from * 3 times more, slip last st in joining st.

**Round 5**: *8dc in next 3-ch sp, ss in same 3-ch sp; rep from * 3 times more, slip last st in joining st.

Fasten off.

## Small flower (make 2)

Using B, make 5ch, join with a ss in first ch to make a ring.

**Round 1**: *1sc, 1dc, 1sc in ring, rep from * 3 times. (4 petals)

**Round 2**: *2ch, from WS ss in base of second sc of next petal (pick up 2 loops); rep from * 3 times more, slip last st in first ss. (4 loops)

Join in C.

**Round 3**: *4dc in next 2ch sp (at back), ss in same ch sp; rep from * 3 times more.

Fasten off.

## Joining braid

Cut six 24in. (60cm) lengths of A and tie in the middle. Taking each side separately, braid the strands until there is approx. 1½in. (4cm) of yarn left at the bottom. Secure the braid with a length of yarn.

## Finishing

Sew in ends.

Position the braid in the center of the reverse of the large flower and secure. Sew a small flower on each end of the braid at the point where you secured each side. Position the large flower on the shoulder of the poncho and sew on.

# Tasseled Baby Poncho

This is a really popular and classic poncho, one of the first crochet projects I ever made. It is an excellent gift or quick project for a baby—you can finish it in one evening!

## Materials

**50% baby alpaca/50% merino mix light worsted (DK) yarn, such as Rooster Almerino DK**

→ 1:**1** x 1¾oz (50g) ball—approx. 124:**124**yds (112.5:**112.5**m)—of green (A)
→ 2:**3** x 1¾oz (50g) balls—approx. 248:**372**yds (225:**337.5**m)—of yellow (B)
→ 1:**1** x 1¾oz (50g) ball—approx. 124:**124**yds (112.5:**112.5**m)—of bright pink (C)
→ E/4 (3.5mm) crochet hook

## Abbreviations

**ch** chain; **dc** double crochet; **inc** increase; **patt** pattern(s); **rep** repeat; **sc** single crochet; **sp** space; **ss** slip stitch; **st(s)** stitch(es)

## Size

**To fit age**: 6–12:**12–18** months

## Finished size

| Length | (in.): | 12 | 15 |
|---|---|---|---|
| | (cm): | 30 | 37.5 |
| Side length | (in.): | 9 | 12 |
| | (cm): | 22.5 | 30 |

## Gauge

5 patt x 9 rows over a 4in. (10cm) square using a E/4 (3.5mm) hook.

## Poncho

Using A, make 72:**88**ch, join with ss to form a ring.

**Round 1**: 1ch, 1sc in each ch to end, ss in first ch with B. (72:**88** sts)
Fasten off A.

**Round 2**: 3ch, 1dc in each of next 2 sts, 1ch, skip 1 st, *1dc in each of next 3 sts, 1ch, skip 1 st; rep from * to end, join with ss in top of first 3-ch.

**Round 3**: Ss in each of next 2 sts, ss in next ch sp, 3ch, [2dc, 1ch, 3dc] in same ch sp, *1ch, 3dc in next ch sp; rep from * 7:**9** times more, 1ch [3dc, 1ch, 3dc] in next ch sp, 1ch, 3dc in next ch sp; rep from * 7:**9** times more, 1ch, ss in top of first 3-dc.

**Round 4**: Ss in each of next 2 sts, ss in next ch sp, 3ch, [2dc, 1ch, 3dc] in same ch sp *1ch, 3dc in next ch sp; rep from * to next inc group from previous round, 1ch [3dc, 1ch, 3dc] in next ch sp (middle of inc group), 1ch, 3dc in next ch sp; rep from * to end of round, 1ch, ss in top of first 3-dc.

Rep Round 4 until 20:**26** rows in total have been worked (or make to required length).
Fasten off.

## Finishing

Sew in ends.

Using C, make approx. 2in. (5cm) tassels by wrapping yarn around four fingers four times. Remove from fingers, cut yarn at bottom, insert top loop into space at bottom of poncho, pull other end through loop forming a tassel and trim.

# Blossom Shawl

An heirloom project with a vintage feel. This shawl is made up from individual motifs and then decorated with little flowers around the edge to give it some movement.

## Materials

**55% merino/45% silk mix sportweight (4-ply) yarn, such as  Fyberspates Scrumptious 4-ply**

➜ 5 x 3½oz (100g) skeins—approx. 1995yds (1825m) of beige (MC)

➜ Small amount of various shades of pink (CC)

➜ D/3 (3mm) crochet hook

## Abbreviations

**CC** contrast color; **ch** chain; **ch sp** chain space; **dc** double crochet; **hdc** half double crochet; **MC** main color; **rep** repeat; **sc** single crochet; **sp** space; **ss** slip stitch; **st(s)** stitch(es); **yo** yarn over hook

## Special abbreviations

**3chpicot** (3-chain picot) work 3ch, ss in third chain from hook, pull tight

**dcCl** (double crochet cluster) *yo, insert hook into ring, yo, pull yarn through, yo, pull yarn through 2 loops; rep from * twice more (4 loops on hook), yo, pull yarn through all 4 loops (1dc cluster made)

## Finished size

Approx. 44 x 35in. (112 x 89cm)

## Main motif (make 86)

Using MC, make 8ch, join with ss in first ch to make a ring.

**Round 1**: 3ch, *yo, insert hook through ring, yo, pull yarn through, yo, pull yarn through 2 loops (2 loops on hook); rep from * once more (3 loops on hook), yo, draw yarn through all 3 loops, **5ch, 1dcCl into ring; repeat from ** 10 times more. (12 clusters)

**Round 2**: 2ch, 1dc in the top of first dcCl, 1ch, * make a 3chpicot, 5ch, 1sc in top of next dcCl; rep from * 11 times more, ss in 1-ch at top of first dcCl from previous round.

**Round 3**: Take yarn behind 3chpicot and ss in second ch of 5-ch arch, 3ch (counts as 1dc), 4dc in 5-ch sp, *5ch, [5dc in next 5-ch sp] twice; rep from * 4 times more, 5ch, 5dc in next 5-ch sp, ss into top of first 3-ch.

**Round 4**: Skip first st, sc in next st, 5dc in next 5-ch sp, 1ch, 3chpicot, 5dc in same 5-ch sp,

skip 2 sts, sc in next st, *7ch, skip 4 sts, 1sc in next st, 5dc in 5-ch sp, 1ch, 3chpicot, 5dc in same 5-ch sp, skip 2 sts, 1sc in next st, rep from * 4 times more, 7ch, skip 3 sts, ss in next st.

Fasten off.

### Small flowers (make 28 in assorted shades)

Using CC, make 4ch, join with ss in first ch to make a ring.

6sc in ring.

*Ss in first sc, 3ch, 1dc in same st, 3ch, ss in same st; rep from * 5 times more. (6 petals)

Fasten off.

### Finishing

Lay out a row of 10 main motifs, followed by a row of 9 main motifs; repeat this sequence three more times and finish with another row of 10 motifs.

Sew the main motifs together at the points and middle chain between points.

Position and stitch a flower on each point along the long edge of the shawl and in the middle of the center motif of the curve on the short edge.

# Toggle Jacket

The pretty star stitch on this jacket makes it a really special piece of clothing. The yarn is soft and really works well in this lovely color.

## Back

Make 58:**63**:69:**75**ch.

**Row 1**: 1sc in next ch from hook, 1sc in each ch to end. (56:**62**:68:**74** sts)

**Row 2**: SS1, SS2 to last st, 1hdc in top of 3-ch from previous row. (27:**30**:33:**36** stars)

**Row 3**: 3ch, *2dc in center of star; rep from * to end, 1hdc in last st of last star of Row 2.

   Rep Rows 2 and 3 until a total of 15:**15**:17:**19** rows have been worked.

**Next row**: Rep Row 2.

### Back shaping for armhole:

**Row 1**: 3ch, skip first star stitch, *2dc in center of next star; rep from * to last star, skip last star, 1hdc in top of last st.

**Row 2**: SS1, SS2 to last st, 1hdc in top of 3-ch from previous row. (25:**28**:31:**34** stars)

Rep Rows 1 and 2 another 3:**4**:5:**6** times more. (19:**20**:21:**22** stars)

**Row 9**: Rep Row 1.

   Fasten off.

## Left front

Make 33:**37**:39:**43**ch.

**Row 1**: 1sc in next ch from hook, 1sc in each ch to end. (32:**36**:38:**42** sts)

**Row 2**: SS1, SS2 to last st, 1hdc in top of sc from previous row. (15:**17**:18:**20** stars)

**Row 3**: 3ch, *2dc in center of star; rep from * to end, 1hdc in last st of last star of Row 2.

   Rep Rows 2 and 3 until a total of 15:**15**:17:**19** rows have been worked.

**Next row**: Rep Row 2.

## Materials

**50% baby alpaca/50% merino light worsted (DK) yarn, such as Rooster Almerino Baby**

→ 3:3:4:4 x 1¾oz (50g) balls—approx. 408:**408**:544:**544**yds (375:**375**:500:**500**m)—of green

→ E/4 (3.5mm) crochet hook

→ 3 x wooden toggle buttons each ¾in. (2cm) long

## Abbreviations

**beg** beginning; **ch** chain; **dc** double crochet; **hdc** half double crochet; **rep** repeat; **RS** right side; **sc** single crochet; **sc2tog** (single crochet 2 together decrease) insert hook in next st, yo, pull yarn through (2 loops on hook). Without finishing st, insert hook in next st, yo, pull yarn through (3 loops on hook), yo, pull yarn through all 3 loops on hook; **ss** slip stitch; **st(s)** stitch(es); **WS** wrong side; **yo** yarn over hook

## Special abbreviations

**SS1** (Star Stitch 1) 3ch, insert hook in second ch from hook, pull yarn through, insert hook in third ch from hook, pull yarn through, insert hook in next st, pull loop through (4 loops on hook). Insert hook in next st, pull yarn through, insert hook in next st, pull yarn through (6 loops on hook), yo, pull yarn through all 6 loops, 1ch

**SS2** (Star Stitch 2) insert hook in base of ch just made, pull yarn through, insert hook in front of last st of previous star stitch, pull yarn through, insert hook in whole of same st, pull yarn through, insert hook in next st, pull yarn through, insert hook in next st, pull yarn through (6 loops), yo, pull yarn through all 6 loops, 1ch

## Size

**To fit age**: 3–6:**6–12**:12–18:**24–36** months

## Finished size

| | | | | | |
|---|---|---|---|---|---|
| Chest | (in.): | 21 | **23** | 25 | **27** |
| | (cm): | 52.5 | **57.5** | 62.5 | **67.5** |
| Length | (in.): | 10 | **11** | 12 | **13** |
| | (cm): | 25 | **27.5** | 30 | **32.5** |
| Sleeve seam | (in.): | 5 | **7** | 9 | **11** |
| | (cm): | 12.5 | **17.5** | 22.5 | **27.5** |

## Gauge

11 stars x 5½ star patterns over a 4in. (10cm) square using a E/4 (3.5mm) hook.

**Shaping for left front armhole:**
**Row 1:** With WS facing, 3ch *2dc in center of next star from previous row; rep from * to last star, skip last star, 1hdc in top of star of previous row.
**Row 2:** SS1, SS2 to end of row, 1hdc in top of 3-ch from previous row. (14:**16**:17:**19** stars)
   Rep last 2 rows 3:**4**:5:**6** times more.
**Row 9:** Rep Row 1.
   Fasten off.

**Right front**
Make 33:**37**:39:**43**ch.
**Row 1:** 1sc in next ch from hook, 1sc in each ch to end. (32:**36**:38:**42** sts)
**Row 2:** SS1, SS2 to last st, 1hdc in top of sc from previous row. (15:**17**:18:**20** stars)
**Row 3:** 3ch, skip 1 star, *2dc in center of next star; rep from * to end, 1hdc in top of last st of last star of Row 2.
   Rep Rows 2 and 3 until a total of 15:**15**:17:**19** rows have been worked.
**Next row:** Rep Row 2.
**Shaping for right front armhole:**
**Row 1:** With WS facing, 3ch, skip 1 star, *2dc in center of each star from previous row; rep from * to end, 1hdc in last st of star of previous row.
**Row 2:** SS1, SS2 to end of row, 1hdc in top of 3-ch from previous row. (14:**16**:17:**19** stars)

Rep last 2 rows 3:**4**:5:**6** times more.
**Row 9:** Rep Row 1.
Fasten off.

**Sleeves (make 2)**
Make 39:**41**:43:**45**ch.
**Row 1:** 1sc in next ch from hook, 1sc in each ch to end. (38:**40**:42:**44** sts)
**Row 2:** SS1, SS2 to end of row, 1hdc in top of 3-ch from previous row. (18:**19**:20:**21** stars)
**Row 3:** 3ch, *2dc in center of star from previous row; rep from * to last star, skip last star, 1hdc in top of star of previous row.
   Rep last 2 rows 5:**8**:10:**13** times more.
**Next row:** Rep Row 2.
**Armhole shaping for sleeve:**
**Row 15:** 3ch, skip one star stitch, *2dc in center of next star; rep from * to last star stitch, skip last star stitch, 1hdc in top of 3-ch from previous row.
**Row 16:** SS1, SS2 to end of row, 1hdc in top of 3-ch from previous row. (16:**17**:18:**19** stars)
   Rep last 2 rows 3:**4**:5:**6** times more.
(10:**9**:8:**7** stars)
   Rep Row 15.
   Fasten off.
   Sew side and sleeve seams, fit sleeves.

**Neck edging**
With RS facing, join yarn at top of right front neck edge, 1sc in each of next 16:**18**:19:**21** sts (to beg of first sleeve top), [sc2tog, 1sc in each of next 4:**5**:5:**6** sts] three times, sc2tog, 1sc in each of next 4:**1**:2:**2** sts, [sc2tog, 1sc in each of next  5 sts] 3:**4**:4:**4** times, 1sc in each of next 2:**1**:1:**2** sts, [sc2tog, 1sc in each of next 4:**5**:5:**6** sts] three times, sc2tog, 1sc in each st across left front, turn.
**Next row:** 1ch, 1sc in each of next 16:**18**:19:**21** sts (front), sc2tog over next 16:**18**:20:**22** sts (sleeve), sc2tog, 1sc in each of next 20:**26**:27:**28** sts (back), sc2tog, sc2tog over next 16:**18**:20:**22** sts (second sleeve), 1sc

in each of next 16:**18**:19:**21** sts (front).
(70:**80**:87:**94** sts)
   Do not fasten off.

**Collar:**
**Row 1:** 2ch, 1hdc in each st. (70:**80**:87:**94** sts)
**Row 2:** 2ch, skip 1 st, 1hdc in each of next 9:**10**:11:**13** sts, 2hdc in next st, 1hdc in each of next 10:**12**:13:**14** sts, 2hdc in next st, 1hdc in each of next 10:**12**:13:**14** sts, 2hdc in next st, 1hdc in each of next 10:**12**:13:**14** sts, 2hdc in next st, 1hdc in each of next 10:**12**:13:**14** sts, 2hdc in next st, 1hdc in each of next 9:**10**:11:**13** sts, skip 1 st, 1hdc in 2-ch from previous row.
**Row 3:** 2ch, skip 1 st, 1hdc in each of next 9:**10**:11:**13** sts, 2hdc in next st, 1hdc in each of next 11:**12**:13:**14** sts, 2hdc in next st, 1hdc in each of next 11:**12**:13:**14** sts, 2hdc in next st, 1hdc in each of next 11:**12**:13:**14** sts, 2hdc in next st, 1hdc in each of next 11:**12**:13:**14** sts, 2hdc in next st, 1hdc in each of next 9:**10**:12:**13** sts, skip 1 st, 1hdc in 2-ch from previous row.
**Row 4:** 2ch, skip 1 st, 1hdc in each st to last 2 sts, skip 1 st, 1hdc in 2-ch from previous row.
**Row 5:** Rep Row 4.
**Row 6:** 2ch, skip 1 st, 1hdc in each of next 5:**6**:7:**9** sts, 2hdc in next st, 1hdc in each of next 12:**13**:14:**15** sts, 2hdc in next st, 1hdc in each of next 12:**13**:14:**15** sts, 2hdc in next st, 1hdc in each of next 12:**13**:14:**15** sts, 2hdc in next st, 1hdc in each of next 12:**13**:14:**15** sts, 2hdc in next st, 1hdc in each of next 8:**9**:10:**12** sts, skip 1 st, 1hdc in 2-ch from previous row.
**Row 7:** 1ch, skip 1 st, 1sc in each st to last 2 sts, skip 1 st, ss in 2-ch from previous row.
   Fasten off.

**Finishing**
Sew in ends. Sew on toggle buttons.
**Toggle loops (make one for each button):**
Make 16ch. Fasten off.
   Fold chain in half to make a loop and sew two ends onto jacket on opposite front edge to correspond with toggle buttons.

# Petal Cape

A really sweet little cape made using an open shell stitch on the petals and a "crocodile stitch" collar making scales or scallops around the neck.

## Materials

**50% baby alpaca/50% merino light worsted (DK) yarn, such as Rooster Almerino Baby**

➔ 3:**4**:5 x 1¾oz (50g) balls—approx. 408:**544**:680yds (375:**500**:625m)—of red (A)

**50% baby alpaca/50% merino mix light worsted (DK) yarn, such as Rooster Almerino DK**

➔ 1 x 1¾oz (50g) ball—approx. 124yds (112.5m)—of pale pink (B)

➔ E/4 (3.5mm) crochet hook

## Abbreviations

**ch** chain; **dc** double crochet; **patt** pattern; **rep** repeat; **RS** right side; **sc** single crochet; **sp** space; **ss** slip stitch; **st(s)** stitch(es); **yo** yarn over hook

## Size

**To fit age**: 3–12:**18–24**:24–36 months

## Finished size

| | | | | |
|---|---|---|---|---|
| Circumference | (in.): | 30½ | **34¼** | 38 |
| | (cm): | 76.5 | **86.5** | 95 |
| Length | (in.): | 12 | **14** | 14¾ |
| | (cm): | 30 | **35** | 37 |

## Gauge

3½ shell patterns x 8 rows over a 4in. (10cm) square using a E/4 (3.5mm) hook.

## Main body

Using A, make 91:**99**:107ch.

**Row 1**: 1dc in 3rd ch from hook, *1ch, skip 2 ch, [1dc, 3ch, 1dc] in next ch, 1ch, skip 2 ch, 1dc in each of next 3 ch; rep from * to end, omitting 1dc at end of last rep. (89:**97**:105 sts)

**Row 2**: 4ch (counts as 1dc, 1ch), 7dc in next 3-ch sp, *1ch, skip 2 dc, 1dc in next dc, 1ch, 7dc in next 3-ch sp; rep from * to last 3 dc, 1ch, skip 2 dc, 1dc in top of 3-ch.

**Row 3**: 4ch, 1dc in base of 4-ch, 1ch, skip 2 dc, 1dc in each of next 3 dc, *1ch, skip 2 dc, [1dc, 3ch, 1dc] in next dc, 1ch, skip 2 dc, 1dc in each of next 3 dc; rep from * to last 3 dc, skip 2 dc, [1dc, 1ch, 1dc] in third of 4-ch from previous row.

**Row 4**: 3ch (counts as 1dc), 3dc in first ch sp, 1ch, skip 2 dc, 1dc in next dc, *1ch, 7dc in next 3-ch sp, 1ch, skip 2 dc, 1dc in next dc; rep from * to last 3 dc, 1ch, skip 2 dc, 3dc in last ch sp, 1dc in third of 4-ch from previous row.

**Row 5**: 3ch, skip 1 dc, 1dc in next dc, *1ch,

skip 2 dc, [1dc, 3ch, 1dc] in next dc, 1ch, skip 2 dc, 1dc in each of next 3 dc; rep from * to end, omitting one dc at end of last rep and placing last dc in third of 3-ch from previous row.

**Row 6**: 4ch (counts as 1dc, 1ch), 9dc in next 3-ch sp, * 2ch, skip 3 dc, 1dc in next dc, 2ch, 9dc in next 3-ch sp; rep from * to last 3 dc, 2ch, skip 2 dc, 1dc in top of 3-ch.

**Row 7**: 4ch, 1dc in base of 4-ch, 2ch, skip 3 dc, 1dc in each of next 3 dc, * 2ch, skip 2 dc [1dc, 3ch, 1dc] in next dc, 2ch, skip 3 dc, 1dc in each of next 3 dc; rep from * to last 3 dc, 2ch, skip 3 dc, [1dc, 1ch, 1dc] in third of 4-ch.

**Row 8**: 3ch (counts as 1dc), 3dc in first ch sp, 2ch, skip 2 dc, 1dc in next dc, * 2ch, 9dc in next 3-ch sp, 2ch, skip 2 dc, 1dc in next dc; rep from * to last 3 dc, 2ch, skip 2 dc, 3dc in last ch sp, 1dc in third of 4-ch.

**Row 9**: 3ch, skip 1 dc, 1dc in next dc, 2ch, skip 2 dc, [1dc, 3ch, 1dc] in next dc, * 2ch, skip 3 dc, 1dc in each of next 3 dc, 2ch, skip 3 dc, [1dc, 3ch, 1dc] in next dc; rep from * to last 3 dc, make 2ch, skip 1 dc, 1dc in each of next 2 dc, 1dc in third of 4-ch.

**Row 10**: Rep Row 6.

**Row 11**: 4ch, 1dc in base of 4-ch, 2ch, skip 3 dc, 1dc in next dc, 2dc in next dc, 1dc in next dc, *2ch, skip 3 dc, [1dc, 3ch, 1dc] in next dc, 2ch, skip 3 dc, 1dc in next dc, 2dc in next dc, 1dc in next dc; rep from * to last 3 dc, 2ch, skip 3 dc, [1dc, 1ch, 1dc] in third of 4-ch from previous row.

**Row 12**: 3ch, 3dc in first ch sp, 2ch, skip 2 dc, 1dc in each of next 2 dc, skip 1 dc, * 2ch, 9dc in next 3-ch sp, 2ch, skip 1 dc, 1dc in each of next 2 dc, skip 1 dc; rep from * to last 2-ch sp, 2ch skip 2-ch sp, 3dc in last 4-ch sp, 1dc in top of 3-ch from previous row.

**Row 13**: 3ch, skip 1 dc, 1dc in next dc, 2ch,

skip 2 dc, *1dc in next dc, 5ch, 1dc in next dc, 2ch, **skip 3 dc, 1dc in next dc, 2dc in next dc, 1dc in next dc, 2ch, skip 3 dc; rep from * to last rep, ending at **, skip 1 dc, 1dc in each of next 3 dc, 1dc in top of 3-ch from previous row.

**Row 14**: 5ch, 11dc in next 5-ch sp, * 3ch, skip 1 dc, 1dc in each of next 2 dc, skip 1 dc, 3ch, 11dc in next 5-ch sp; rep from * to last dc, 2ch, skip 1 dc, 1dc in top of 3-ch from previous row.

**Row 15**: 5ch, 1dc in base of 5-ch, *3ch, skip 4 dc, 1dc in next dc, 2dc in next dc, 1dc in next dc, skip 4 dc, 3ch, 1dc in next dc, 5ch, 1dc in next dc; rep from * to last 11 dc from previous row, skip 4 dc, 3ch, 1dc in next dc, 2dc in next dc, 1dc in next dc, skip 4 dc, 3ch, 1dc in 3rd of 5-ch from previous row.

**Sizes 18–24:24–36 months only:**

**Row 16**: 3ch, 4dc in first ch sp, 3ch, skip 1 dc, 1dc in each of next 2 dc, skip 1 dc, * 3ch, 11dc in next 5-ch sp, 3ch, skip 1 dc, 1dc in each of next 2 dc, skip 1 dc; rep from * to last 3-ch sp, 3ch skip 3-ch sp, 4dc in last 5-ch sp.

**Row 17**: 3ch, skip 1 dc, 1dc in next dc, 3ch, skip 2 dc, *1dc in next dc, 5ch, 1dc in next dc, 3ch, **skip 4 dc, 1dc in next dc, 2dc in next dc, 1dc in next dc, 3ch, skip 4 dc; rep from * to last rep, ending at **, skip 2 dc, 1dc in each of next 3 dc, 1dc in top of 3-ch from previous row.

**Row 18**: 5ch, 11dc in next 5-ch sp, * 3ch, skip 1 dc, 1dc in each of next 2 dc, skip 1 dc, 3ch, 11dc in next 5-ch sp; rep from * to last dc, 2ch, skip 1 dc, 1dc in top of 3-ch from previous row.

**Row 19**: 5ch, 1dc in base of 5-ch, * 3ch, skip 4 dc, 1dc in next dc, 2dc in next dc, 1dc in next dc, skip 4 dc, 3ch, 1dc in next dc, 5ch, 1dc in next dc; rep from * to last 11 dc from previous row, skip 4 dc, 3ch, 1dc in next dc, 2dc in next dc, 1dc in next dc, skip 4 dc, 3ch, 1dc in third of 5-ch from previous row.

Do not fasten off.

**Outer petals 1, 9, and 10:**

**Row 1 (RS facing)**: 7ch, 1sc in first dc, *3ch, skip 1 st, 1sc in next st; rep from * 7 times more, 4ch, skip 1 st, 1dc in next st, turn.

**Row 2**: 7ch, 1sc in next 3-ch sp, *3ch, 1sc in next ch sp; rep from * 6 times more, 4ch, 1dc in third ch of 7-ch from previous row.

**Row 3**: 7ch, 1sc in next 3-ch sp, *3ch, 1sc in next ch sp; rep from * 5 times more, 4ch, 1dc in third ch of 7-ch from previous row.

**Row 4**: 7ch, 1sc in next 3-ch sp, *3ch, 1sc in next ch sp; rep from * 4 times more, 4ch, 1dc in third ch of 7-ch from previous row.

**Row 5**: 7ch, 1sc in next 3-ch sp, *1sc in next ch sp; rep from * 3 times more, 4ch, 1dc in third ch of 7-ch from previous row.

**Row 6**: 7ch, 1sc in next 3-ch sp, *3ch, 1sc in next ch sp; rep from * twice more, 4ch, 1dc in third ch of 7-ch from previous row.

**Row 7**: 7ch, 1sc in next 3-ch sp, *3ch, 1sc in next ch sp; rep from * once more, 4ch, 1dc in third ch of 7-ch from previous row.

**Row 8**: 7ch, 1sc in next 3-ch sp, 4ch, 1dc in third ch of 7-ch from previous row.

**Row 9**: 7ch, 1dc in sc, 4ch, 1dc in third ch of 7-ch from previous row.

**Row 10**: 3ch, 1tr in dc, 3ch, ss in third ch of 5-ch from previous row.

Fasten off.

**Inner petals 2–7:**

**Row 1**: 5ch, 1dc in base of 5-ch, 4ch, skip 2 sts, 1sc in next st, *3ch, skip 1 st, 1sc in next st; rep from * 7 times more. 4ch, skip 2 sts, 1dc in each of next 2 sts, 5ch, turn.

**Row 2**: 1dc in base of 5-ch from previous row, 4ch, 1sc in next 3-ch sp, * 3ch, 1sc in next 3-ch sp; rep from * 6 times more. 4ch, 1dc in next dc, 1dc in third of 5-ch from previous row, 5ch, turn.

**Row 3**: 1dc in base of 5-ch from previous row, 4ch, 1sc in next 3-ch sp, * 3ch, 1sc in next 3-ch sp; rep from * 5 times more, 4ch, 1dc in next st, 1dc in third of 5-ch from previous row, 5ch, turn.

Cont as above having one 3-ch sp less on each row until one 3-ch sp remains, ending each row with 5ch.

**Next row**: 1dc in base of 5-ch, 4ch, 1sc in next 3-ch sp, 4ch, 1dc in next dc, 1dc in third of 5-ch from previous row.

**Next row**: 5ch, 1dc in base of first 5-ch, 3ch, 1dc in next sc, 3ch, 1dc in next dc, 1dc in third of 5-ch.

**Next row**: 5ch, 1dc in base of first 5-ch, 3ch, 1tr in center dc, 3ch, 1ss in third of 5-ch.

Fasten off.

With RS facing, join in same stitch as last ss from previous petal and rep Petal 2.

**Petal 8:**
With RS facing, join yarn in next st from ss from previous petal. Rep Petal 1.

**Collar**
Using A, make 82:**90**:98ch.

**Row 1**: 1sc in second ch from hook, 1sc in each ch to end. (81:**89**:97 sts)

**Row 2**: 3ch (counts as first dc), 1dc in base of first 3-ch, *2ch, skip next 2 sts, 1dc in each of next 2 sts; rep from * to end, 1ch. Do not turn.

**Row 3**: Yo, insert hook in space between 2-dc group from previous row, from behind and from back of work to front, make 5dc in same space (if you turn work to the side, it's easier to make the stitch), 1ch, turn.

Yo, insert hook from left to right (when row of sc is at bottom) and round back of second dc stalk, make 5dc around second dc stem. (1 scale made)

*Skip next 2-dc group, insert hook around first stalk of next dc group (back to front), work 5dc, 1ch, insert hook from left to right and round the stalk of second dc, make 5dc around stalk; rep from * to end of row, turn.

**Row 4**: 3ch, 1dc in base of 3-ch, *2ch. 2dc in the center of scale from previous row, 2ch, 2dc in center of 2-dc group from row 2; rep from * to end scale, 2ch, make 2dc in top edge of last scale, 1ch.

**Row 5**: Yo, insert hook in space between 2-dc group from previous row, from behind and from back of work to front, make 5dc in same space. (if you turn work to the side, it's easier to make the stitch), 1ch, turn.

Yo, insert hook from left to right (when row of sc is at bottom) and round back of second dc stalk, make 5dc around second dc stalk. (1 scale made)

*Skip next 2-dc group, insert hook around first stalk of next dc group (back to front), work 5dc, 1ch, insert hook from left to right and round stalk of second dc, make 5dc around stalk; rep from * to end, make 1ss between last 2dc-group.

**Row 6**: 3ch, 1dc in base of 3-ch, *2ch. 2dc in center of scale from previous row, 2ch, 2dc in center of 2-dc group from 2 rows before; rep from * to end, ss in last center of scale, 1ch, turn.

**Row 7**: Rep Row 3.

**Size 24–36 months only:**
Rep Rows 4–5 once more.
  Fasten off.

**Tie**
Using A and yarn doubled, make a chain approx. 30in. (75cm) long.
  Fasten off.

**Finishing**
Fit collar around neck edge and sew in place. Thread tie on wrong side of collar by weaving in and out of dc groups. Using B, make two small pompoms and attach one on each end of tie.

# Pink Baby Dress

Made in a light, soft yarn with a mix of alpaca and merino wool, this baby dress is easy to wear and embellished with a row of pretty flowers.

## Materials

**50% baby alpaca/50% merino light worsted (DK) yarn, such as Rooster Almerino Baby**

➔ 4 x 1¾oz (50g) balls—approx. 544yds (500m)—of pink (A)

➔ Scraps of off-white (B) and green (C)

➔ D/3 (3mm) and E/4 (3.5mm) crochet hooks

➔ 3 small buttons

## Abbreviations

**ch** chain; **dc** double crochet; **rep** repeat; **RS** right side; **sc** single crochet; **sp** space; **ss** slip stitch; **st(s)** stitch(es)

## Size

**To fit age**: 6–9 months

## Finished size

**Chest**: 22in. (55cm)

**Length**: 14½in. (36.5cm)

## Gauge

4 shells x 6 rows of pattern over a 4in. (10cm) square using a E/4 (3.5mm) hook.

## Yoke

Using A and E/4 (3.5mm) hook throughout, make 61ch.

**Row 1**: 1dc in fourth ch from hook, 1dc in each of next 57ch. (58 sts)

**Row 2**: 3ch, skip 1 st, 1dc in each of next 5 sts, *2dc in next st, 1dc in each of next 3 sts; rep from * 11 times more, 1dc in each of next 4 sts, 1dc in top of turning ch. (70 sts)

**Row 3**: 3ch, skip 1 st, 1dc in each of next 5 sts, *2dc in next st, 1dc in each of next 4 sts; rep from * 11 times more, 1dc in each of next 4 sts, 1dc in top of turning ch. (82 sts)

**Row 4**: 3ch, skip 1 st, 1dc in each of next 5 sts, *2dc in next st, 1dc in each of next 5 sts; rep from * 11 times more, 1dc in each of next 4 sts, 1dc in top of turning ch. (94 sts)

**Row 5**: 3ch, skip 1 st, 1dc in each of next 5 sts, *2dc in next st, 1dc in each of next 6 sts; rep from * 11 times more, 1dc in each of next 4 sts, 1dc in top of turning ch. (106 sts)

**Row 6**: 3ch, skip 1 st, 1dc in each of next 5 sts, *2dc in next st, 1dc in each of next 7 sts; rep from * 11 times more, 1dc in each of next 4 sts, 1dc in top of turning ch. (118 sts)

**Row 7**: 3ch, skip 1 st, 1dc in each of next 2 sts, 2dc in next st, 1dc in each of next 2 sts, 2dc in next st, *1dc in each of next 8 sts, 2dc in the next st; rep from * 4 times more. 1dc in each of next 3 sts, 2dc in next st, 1dc in each of next 4 sts, 2dc in next st, * 1dc in each of next 8 sts, 2dc in next st; rep from * 5 times more, 1dc in each of next 3 sts, 1dc in top of turning ch. (133 sts)

Do not fasten off.

## Skirt:

With RS facing, 1sc in each of next 21 sts, make 7ch loosely, skip 25 sts (for sleeve), 1sc in each of next 20 sts, 2sc in next st, 1sc in each of next 19 sts (for back), make 7ch loosely, skip 25 sts, 1sc in each of next 21 sts.

### Commence pattern:

**Row 1**: 1ch, 1sc in next st, skip 1 st, *[1dc, 2ch, 1dc, 2ch, 1dc] in next st, skip 1 st, 1sc in next st, skip 1 st; rep from * to last st, 1sc in last st.

**Row 2**: 4ch (for first dc and space), 1dc back in first st, *1sc in dc in center of group from previous row, [1dc, 2ch, 1dc, 2ch, 1dc] in next sc; rep from * to last group, 1sc in dc in center of group from previous row, [1dc, 2ch, 1dc] in last sc.

**Row 3**: 1ch, 1sc back in last dc from end of previous row, *[1dc, 2ch, 1dc, 2ch, 1dc] in next sc, 1sc in center of group; rep from * to end, 1sc in second ch of 4-ch from previous row.

Repeat Rows 2 and 3 of pattern until work

measures approx. 14½in. (36.5cm) from shoulder (or until required length).

Fasten off.

## Sleeves (make two)

With RS facing, attach yarn to middle stitch of underarm.

**Round 1**: 3ch, 36dc evenly around armhole, ss in top of first 3-ch. (36 sts)

**Round 2**: 3ch, 1dc in each st to end, ss in top of first 3-ch.

**Round 3**: 2ch, 1sc in each st, ss in top of first 2-ch.

**Round 4**: Rep Round 3.

Fasten off.

## Flowers

Using B and D/3 (3mm) hook, make 4ch, join with a ss in first ch to make a ring.

*3ch, 1dc in ring, 3ch, ss in ring; rep from * until 5 petals are made.

Fasten off. Using a yarn needle use loose end and weave around center to make circle closed.

Using C, make a French knot in the center, wrapping wool around needle 5 times.

## Finishing

Sew back seam up to yoke using either backstitch or overstitch.

Attach flowers over the yoke join at front of dress.

Sew 3 buttons onto back of yoke to line up with holes in the double crochet stitches.

Sew in ends.

# Toddler Dress

This is great as an overdress worn over leggings or thick tights. It has a pretty flared skirt and the buttons are crocheted using a fine cotton.

## Materials

**50% baby alpaca/50% merino light worsted (DK) yarn, such as Rooster Almerino Baby**

→ 5 x 1¾oz (50g) balls—approx. 680yds (625m)—of blue (A)

**100% cotton 6-ply crochet thread, such as Anchor Aida 6-ply crochet cotton No.5**

→ 1 x 1¾oz (50g) ball—approx. 219yds (200m)—of dark blue (B)

→ B/1 (2mm), E/4 (3.5mm), F/5 (4mm), and I/9 (5.5mm) crochet hooks

→ 80in. (2m) navy blue ½in. (1cm) wide velvet ribbon

## Abbreviations

**ch** chain(s); **dc** double crochet; **hdc** half double crochet; **rep** repeat ; **RS** right side; **sc** single crochet; **sc2tog** (single crochet 2 together decrease) insert hook in next st, yo, pull yarn through (2 loops on hook). Without finishing st, insert hook in next st, yo, pull yarn through (3 loops on hook), yo, pull yarn through all 3 loops on hook; **sp** space; **ss** slip stitch; **st(s)** stitch(es); **yo** yarn over hook

## Special abbreviations

**Picot 1** 3ch, ss in first of 3ch, ss into same st as 3-ch, skip 1 st, ss in next st

**Picot 2** 3ch, [1sc, 3ch, 1sc] in next sc

**V-st** 1dc, 1ch, 1dc

## Size

**To fit age**: 18–24:**24–36** months

## Finished size

| Chest | (in.): | 22 | 24 |
|---|---|---|---|
| | (cm): | 55 | 60 |
| Length | (in.): | 18½ | 20½ |
| | (cm): | 46.5 | **51.5** |

## Gauge

5 patterns across x 3 patterns down over a 4in. (10cm) square using a F/5 (4mm) hook.

## Bodice

Using A and F/5 (4mm) hook, make
101:**109**ch.

**Row 1**: 1dc in fourth ch from hook, 1dc in
each of next 3 ch, *1ch, skip next 3 ch, 3dc in
next ch; rep from * to last 7 ch, 1ch, skip next
3 ch, 1dc in each of next 4 ch. 23½:**25½**in.
(59:**64**cm) across.

**Row 2**: 3ch (counts as 1dc) skip first dc, *1dc
in each of next 3 dc, 1ch; rep from * to last 4
dc, 1dc in each of next 3 dc, 1dc in top of 3-ch
from previous row.

**Row 3**: 3ch, skip 1dc, 1dc in each of next 3
dc, 1ch, 1dc in next dc, 1ch, skip next dc, *V-
st in next ch sp, 1ch, skip next 3 dc; rep from
* until last 6 dc, 1ch, skip 2 dc, 1dc in next dc,
1ch, 1dc in each of next 3 sts, 1dc in top of 3-
ch from previous row.

**Row 4**: 3ch, skip 1dc, 1dc in each of next 3
dc, *1ch, skip next V-st, 3dc in next ch sp; rep
from * to last ch sp, skip 1ch sp, 1ch, 1dc in
each of next 3 dc, 1dc in top of 3-ch from
previous row.

**Rows 5–7**: Rep Rows 2–4.

## Divide for armhole, Front yoke:

**Row 1**: 3ch, skip 1dc, *1dc in each of next 3
dc, 1ch; rep from * 4:**5** times more ending
with 1dc in last dc, turn (armhole side).

**Row 2**: 3ch, skip 4 dc, *V-st in next ch sp, 1ch;
rep from * until 6 sts rem, 1ch, skip 2 dc, 1dc
in next dc, 1ch, 1dc in each of next 3 dc, 1dc
in top of 3-ch from previous row.

**Row 3**: 3ch, skip 1dc, 1dc in each of next 3
dc, 1ch, 3dc in next ch sp, *1ch, skip next V-
st, 3dc in next ch sp; rep from * until 3:**4**
groups are completed, ending with 1ch, skip
next V-st, 1dc in top of 3-ch.

**Row 4**: 3ch, skip 1dc, 1ch, *1dc in each of
next 3 dc, 1ch; rep from * once:**twice** more,
1dc in each of next 2dc.

Row 5: 4ch, [V-st in next ch sp, 1ch] twice:**three** times, V-st in top of 3-ch.

Row 6: 3ch, [skip V-st, 3dc in next ch sp, 1ch] twice, V-st in next ch sp.

Row 7: 3ch, skip first dc, 1dc in each dc, 1ch over each ch sp, ending with 1dc in top of 3-ch.

Row 8: Rep Row 7.

Fasten off.

**Back yoke:**

With RS facing, go back to last long row, skip next 4 sts for underarm, attach yarn in next dc.

Row 1: 3ch, *1dc in each of next 3 dc, 1ch; rep from * 10 times more, 1dc in next dc.

Row 2: 4ch, skip 4dc, *V-st in next ch sp, 1ch; rep from * to last 3 dc, skip 2 dc, 1dc in last dc.

Row 3: 3ch, 1dc in first ch sp, 1ch, *skip V-st, 3dc in next ch sp, 1ch; rep from * ending with 2dc in 4-ch sp.

Row 4: 3ch, skip first dc, 1dc in next dc, *1ch, 1dc in each of next 3 dc; rep from * ending

with 1ch, 1dc in last dc, 1dc in top of 3-ch.

Row 5: 4ch, skip 2 dc, *V-st in next ch sp, 1ch; rep from * ending with skip last dc, 1dc in top of 3-ch.

Rows 6–8: Rep Rows 3–5.

Fasten off.

**Second front yoke:**

With RS facing, go back to last long row, skip next 4 sts for underarm, attach yarn in next dc.

Row 1: 3ch, *1dc in each of next 3 dc, 1ch; rep from * 4 times, 1dc in each of next 3 dc, 1dc in top of 3-ch.

Row 2: 3ch, skip 1 dc, 1dc in each of next 3 dc, 1ch, 1dc in next dc, 1ch, skip 2dc, *V-st in next ch sp, 1ch; rep from * three times, skip 3 dc, 1dc in top of 3-ch.

Row 3: 3ch, skip V-st, *3dc in next ch sp, 1ch; rep from * to last 4 dc, skip 1 dc, 1dc in each of next 3 dc, 1dc in top of 3-ch.

Row 4: Ss in each of first 6 sts, 3ch, 1dc in each of next 2 dc, *1dc in each of next 3 dc, 1ch; rep from * once more, 1dc in each of next 2 dc.

Row 5: 3ch, *V-st in first ch, 1ch; rep from * twice more, 1dc in top of 3-ch.

Row 6: 3ch, skip V-st, *3dc in next sp, 1ch; rep from * once more, 2dc in last 3-ch sp.

Row 7: 3ch, *1dc in each dc, 1ch over each ch; rep from * to end, 1dc in top of first 3-ch.

Row 8: Rep Row 7.

Fasten off.


**Skirt**

With RS facing, using A and F/5 (4mm) hook, join yarn in middle st of back bodice.

Round 1: 1ch, 1sc in same sp as ch, 1sc in each of next 4 sts, 2sc in next st, *1sc in each of next 5 sts, 2sc in next st; rep from * 6 times more, 1sc in each of next 11 sts, **2sc in next st, 1sc in each of next 5 sts; rep from ** 7 times more, 1sc in last st, ss in first sc.

Round 2: 5ch, *skip next sc, 1dc in next sc,

1ch; rep from * around to end, ss in fourth of 5-ch. (63 sts)

Round 3: 1ch, 1sc in same ch sp as ss, *1sc in next ch sp, 1sc in next dc; rep from * ending 1sc in last ch sp, join with a ss in first sc. (126 sts)

Round 4: 2ch, 1hdc in next sc, *3ch, skip next sc, 1sc in next sc, 3ch, skip next 2 sc, 1hdc in each of next 2 sc; rep from * ending last rep with 3ch, skip next sc, 1sc in next sc, 3ch, ss in top of first 2-ch.

Round 5: 2ch, 1hdc in next hdc, *3ch, [1sc, 3ch, 1sc] in next sc (picot 2 made), 3ch, skip next 3ch, picot 2 in next sc, 1hdc in each of next 2 hdc; rep from * ending last repeat 3ch, picot 2 in next sc, 3ch, join with a ss in top of 2-ch.

Round 6: 1ch, 1sc in same sp as ch, 1sc in next hdc, 1sc in next ch sp, *5ch, skip 1 picot 2, 1sc in next ch sp, 1sc in each of next 2 hdc, 1sc in next ch sp; rep from * ending with 5ch, 1sc in last ch sp, join with a ss in first sc.

Round 7: 1ch, 1sc in same sp as ch, 1sc in next sc, *skip 1sc, 7sc in 5-ch sp, skip next sc, 1sc in each of next 2 sc; rep from * ending with 7sc in last ch sp, join with a ss in first sc. (189 sts)

Round 8: 3ch (counts as 1dc), 1dc in next sc and in each sc around, join with ss in top of 3-ch. (189 sts)

Round 9: 1ch, 1sc in same sp as ch, 1sc in each dc, join with ss in first sc.

Change to I/9 (5.5mm) hook.

Round 10: 3ch, 1dc in next sc, *3ch, skip next 3 sc, 1sc in next sc, 3ch, skip next 3 sc, 1dc in each of next 2 sc; rep from * ending with 3ch, skip next 3 sc, 1sc in next sc, 3ch, join with a ss in top of 3-ch.

Round 11: 3ch, 1dc in next dc, * 3ch, [1sc, 3ch, 1sc] in next sc (picot 2 made). 3ch, skip next 3ch, picot 2 in next sc, 1dc in each of next 2 dc; rep from * ending last rep 3ch, picot 2 in next sc, 3ch, join with a ss in top of 2-ch.

**Round 12**: Rep Round 6.

**Round 13**: Rep Round 7.

**Round 14**: Rep Round 10.

**Round 15**: Rep Round 11.

**Rounds 16–20**: Rep Rounds 6–10.

**Round 21**: Rep Round 11, working dc instead of hdc.

**Round 22**: Rep Round 6, making 7ch instead of 5ch.

**Round 23**: Rep Round 7, working 9sc instead of 7sc.

**Round 24**: 3ch, 1dc in next sc, * 4ch, skip next 4 sc, 1sc in next sc, 4ch, skip next 4 sc, 1dc in each of next 2 sc; rep from * ending with 4ch, skip next 4 sc, 1sc in next sc, 4ch, join with a ss in top of 3-ch.

**Round 25**: 3ch, 1dc in next dc, * 4ch, picot 2 in next sc, 4ch, skip next 4 ch, 1dc in each of next 2 dc; rep from * ending with 4ch, join with ss in top of 3-ch.

**Round 26**: Rep Round 6, making 7ch instead of 5ch.

**Round 27**: Rep Round 7, working 9sc instead of 7sc.

**Rounds 28–31**: Rep Rounds 24–27.

**Round 32**: Rep Round 8.

Fasten off.

### Sleeves (make two)

Using A and F/5 (4mm) hook, make 34ch.

**Row 1**: 2dc in fourth ch from hook, *1ch, skip next 2-ch, 3dc in next ch; rep from * to end. (11 dc groups)

**Row 2**: 3ch, skip 1dc, 1dc in each of next 2 dc, *1ch, 1dc in each of next 3 dc; rep from * ending 1ch, 1dc in each of last 2 dc, 1dc in top of 3-ch.

### Shaping:

**Row 1**: Ss in each st to first ch sp, ss in first ch sp, 4ch, *V-st in next ch sp, 1ch; rep from * ending 1ch, 1dc in last ch sp. (8 V-sts)

**Row 2**: 3ch, 2dc in first ch sp, *1ch, skip V-st, 3dc in next ch sp; rep from * ending 1ch, 3dc in 4-ch sp.

**Row 3**: 3ch, skip 1dc, 1dc in each of next 2 dc, *1ch, 1dc in each of next 3 dc; rep from * ending 1ch, 1dc in each of last 2 dc, 1dc in top of 3-ch.

**Row 4**: 3ch, skip first 2 dc, V-st, 1ch in each ch sp, ending with 1dc in top of 3-ch.

**Row 5**: 3ch, skip first V-st, *3dc in next ch sp, 1ch; rep from * ending 1dc in top of 3-ch. (7 dc groups)

**Row 6**: 3dc, skip 1 group of 3 dc, *1dc in each of next 3 dc, 1ch; rep from * to last 3 dc group, skip last group, 1dc in top of 3-ch.

**Row 7**: 3ch, skip 1 st, 3dc, V-st, 1ch in each ch sp, ending with 1dc in top of 3-ch.

Fasten off.

### Buttons (make 4)

Using B/1 (2mm) hook and B, make 3ch, join with ss to form a ring.

**Round 1**: 1ch, 2sc in each ch, join with a ss in top of first 2-ch. (6 sts)

**Round 2**: 1ch, 2sc in each st, join with a ss in top of first 2-ch. (12 sts)

Fasten off leaving a long tail, weave sts closed with a yarn needle and pull tight.

### Finishing

Sew sleeves in armholes.

### Sleeve edging:

With RS facing and E/4 (3.5mm) hook, join yarn in st at seam.

Picot 1 around, join with a ss in first 3-ch.

Fasten off.

### Armhole edging and front, back, side edgings:

With RS facing, and E/4 (3.5mm) hook, join yarn at top corner edge.

1sc in each of next 11 sts to sleeve top,

*sc2tog, 1sc in next st; rep from * across top of sleeve, back and second sleeve top, finishing at top left front border.

Fasten off.

With RS facing and E/4 (3.5mm) hook, join yarn at base of right hand front.

1ch, make a picot edging using picot 1 around front, right-hand sleeve top, back, left-hand sleeve top and front up to end of front edging (not down straight edge of front).

Sew buttons in place onto dress front.

Weave ribbon in between spaces at waist, tie in a bow at the front.

# CHAPTER FOUR

# Toys, Accessories, & Room Decorations

# Honey Bunny

Honey Bunny is a pretty lilac rabbit with a cute dress. Made with beautifully soft yarn and safety eyes, she's just the right size to grip and cuddle.

## Materials

**Rabbit**

**50% baby alpaca/50% merino wool mix worsted (Aran) yarn, such as Rooster Almerino Aran**

→ 1 x 1¾oz (50g) ball—approx. 103yds (94m)—of lilac (A)

**50% baby alpaca/50% merino light worsted (DK) yarn, such as Rooster Almerino Baby**

→ Small amount of off-white (B)
→ Small piece white felt
→ Black safety eyes
→ Small amount of black embroidery thread
→ Fiberfill stuffing
→ H/8 (5mm) crochet hook

**Dress**

**50% baby alpaca/50% merino light worsted (DK) yarn, such as Rooster Almerino Baby**

→ 1 x 1¾oz (50g) ball—approx. 136yds (125m)—of off-white (B)
→ Small amounts of pale pink (C) and green (D)
→ Scrap yellow (E)
→ D/3 (3mm) crochet hook

## Abbreviations

**beg** beginning; **ch** chain; **dc** double crochet; **hdc** half double crochet; **rep** repeat; **sc** single crochet; **sc2tog** (single crochet 2 together decrease) insert hook in next st, yo, pull yarn through (2 loops on hook). Without finishing st, insert hook in next st, yo, pull yarn through (3 loops on hook), yo, pull yarn through all 3 loops on hook; **sp** space; **ss** slip stitch; **st(s)** stitch(es); **yo** yarn over hook

## Special abbreviation

**hdc2tog** (half double crochet 2 together decrease) *yo, insert hook in next st, yo, pull yarn through (3 loops on hook). Without finishing st, rep from * in next st (5 loops on hook), yo, pull yarn through all 5 loops on hook

## Finished size

**Length**: approx. 10in. (25cm) tall

## Head

Using A and H/8 (5mm) hook, make 2ch, 4sc in second ch from hook. (4 sts)

Place st marker at beg of each round (loop on hook counts as one st).

**Round 1**: 2sc in each st. (8 sts)

**Round 2**: *1sc in next st, 2sc in next st; rep from * to end of round. (12 sts)

**Rounds 3–4**: 1sc in each st.

**Round 5**: *1sc in each of next 2 sts, 2sc in next st; rep from * to end of round. (16 sts)

**Round 6**: *1sc in each of next 3 sts, 2sc in next st; rep from * to end of round. (20 sts)

**Rounds 7–9**: 1sc in each st. (20 sts)

**Round 10**: *1sc in each of next 3 sts, sc2tog; rep from * to end of round. (16 sts)

**Round 11**: *1sc in each of next 2 sts, sc2tog; rep from * to end of round. (12 sts)

Cut two small white felt circles. Make a small hole in each center, push safety eyes through felt and insert onto face.

Stuff head.

*Use a stitch marker to
mark the beginning and
end of rounds.*

**Round 12:** *1sc in next st, sc2tog; rep from * to end of round. (8 sts)

**Round 13:** Sc2tog around.
   Fasten off.

## Body

Using A and H/8 (5mm) hook, make 2ch, 6sc in second ch from hook.

**Round 1:** 2sc in each st. (12 sts)

**Round 2:** *1sc in next st, 2sc in next st; rep from * to end of round. (18 sts)

**Round 3:** *1sc in each of next 2 sts, 2sc in next st; rep from * to end of round. (24 sts)

**Round 4:** *1sc in each of next 3 sts, 2sc in next st; rep from * to end of round. (30 sts)

**Rounds 5–12:** 1sc in each st.

**Round 13:** *1sc in each of next 3 sts, sc2tog; rep from * to end of round. (24 sts)

**Round 14:** *1sc in each of next 2 sts, sc2tog; rep from * to end of round. (18 sts)

**Round 15:** 1sc in each st.
   Stuff firmly.

**Round 16:** *1sc in next st, sc2tog; rep from * to end of round.

**Round 17:** *1sc, sc2tog; rep from * to end of round.
   Fasten off.

## Ears (make 2)

Using A and H/8 (5mm) hook, make 2ch, 4sc in second ch from hook. (4 sts)

**Round 1:** *1sc in next st, 2sc in next st; rep once more. (6 sts)

**Round 2:** *1sc in next st, 2sc in next st; rep twice more. (9 sts)

**Round 3:** 1sc in each of next 4 sts, 2sc in next st, 1sc in each of next 3 sts, 2sc in last st. (11 sts)

**Rounds 4–10:** 1sc in each st.
   Fasten off.

## Legs (make 2)

Using A and H/8 (5mm) hook, make 2ch, 6sc in second ch from hook.

**Round 1:** 2sc in each st. (12 sts)

**Round 2:** *1sc in each of next 2 sts, 2sc in next st; rep from * to end of round. (16 sts)

**Rounds 3–4:** 1sc in each st.

**Round 5:** *1sc in each of next 2 sts, sc2tog; rep from * to end of round. (12 sts)

**Rounds 6–17:** 1sc in each st.
   Fasten off.

## Arms (make 2)

Using A and H/8 (5mm) hook, make 2ch, 6sc in second ch from hook.

**Round 1:** 2sc in each st. (12 sts)

**Round 2:** *1sc in each of next 2 sts, 2sc in next st; rep from * to end of round. (16 sts)

**Rounds 3–4:** 1sc in each st.

**Round 5:** *1sc in each of next 2 sts, sc2tog; rep from * to end of round. (12 sts)

**Rounds 6–14:** 1sc in each st.
   Fasten off.

## Tail

Using B, make a small pompom by wrapping the yarn around two or three fingers approx. 80 times. Gently slide the yarn off your fingers and tie a knot in the center very securely. The pompom will now have loops on either side of the knot. Cut all the loops; trim and fluff the pompom in shape.

## Making up

Pin and sew body to head. Make a running stitch around the outer edges to make the ears lie flat. Pinch ears at back and sew a slight fold. Pin and sew ears to head. Stuff legs and arms, pin and sew to body. Sew tail to body.

## Dress

Using B and D/3 (3mm) hook, make 48ch, ss in first ch to form a ring.
   Place a stitch marker at beg of round.

**Rounds 1–7:** 1sc in each st. (48 sts)

**Round 8:** Hdc2tog, 1hdc in each st to end. (47 sts)

**Round 9:** Hdc2tog, 1hdc in each st to end. (46 sts)

**Rounds 10–11:** 1hdc in each st to end. (46 sts)

**Round 12:** Hdc2tog, 1hdc in each st to end. (45 sts)

**Round 13:** 1hdc in each st to end. (45 sts)

**Round 14:** Hdc2tog, 1hdc in each st to end. (44 sts)

**Round 15:** Hdc2tog, 1hdc in each st to middle of round, hdc2tog (place stitch marker in dec stitch), 1hdc in each st to end. (There should now be two stitch markers, one to indicate beg of round and one to indicate middle of round.) (42 sts)
   Fasten off.

**Bottom of dress:**

Turn dress upside down, join C to start of round.

**Round 1:** 1sc in each underside of first round of ch.

**Round 2:** *skip 1 st, 5dc in next st, skip 1 st, 1sc in next st; rep from * to end.
   Fasten off.

**Left shoulder:**

Turn dress right way up and work shoulder straps. With fasten off point on your right (under the arm), join B in next st towards center.

1sc in next 3 sts.

*1ch, 1sc in next 3 sts. (3 sts)

1ch, 1sc in next 3 sts. (3 sts)

1ch, sc2tog, 1sc. (2 sts)

1ch, 1sc in next 2 sts. (2 sts)

1ch, sc2tog. (1 st)

1ch.

1sc in ch. (1ch)

2sc in ch. (2 sts)

1ch, 1sc in each st. ( 2 sts)

1ch, 2sc in next st, 1sc in next st. (3 sts)

1ch 1sc in each 3 sts. (3 sts)

1ch. 1sc in each of next 3 sts. (3 sts)

Fasten off.

**Right shoulder:**

Join B on other side 4 sts from first strap.

1sc in each of next 3 sts towards other arm.

Rep from * of Left shoulder.

**Neck edging:**

Using C join yarn in ch where strap is narrowest.

Make 6sc evenly down strap.

1sc in next st, sc2tog in next st, 1sc in next st.

Make 6sc evenly up neck side of other strap.

Join with a ss in ch at top between front and back of strap (top of shoulder), 1ch, turn.

1sc in next 15 sts around neck.

Fasten off.

## Finishing

Sew in ends.

Stitch flowers around dress using D to embroider ch st and E to make French knots for center of flower.

Fit dress on Rabbit and hand sew straps in place at back of dress.

# Coat Hangers

Show off your beautiful baby clothes on these cute hangers. They're much too nice to keep inside a wardrobe.

## Materials

**Watermelons**

**50% baby alpaca/50% merino mix light worsted (DK) yarn, such as Rooster Almerino DK**

➔ 1 x 1¾oz (50g) ball—approx. 124yds (112.5m)—each of yellow (A) and green) (B)

➔ Small amounts of red (C), off-white (D), and black (E)

**Chickens**

**50% baby alpaca/50% merino mix light worsted (DK) yarn, such as Rooster Almerino DK**

➔ 1 x 1¾oz (50g) ball—approx. 124yds (112.5m)—each of green (F) and blue-green (G)

➔ Small amounts of off-white (H), brown (I), yellow (J), and red (K)

**All hangers**

➔ E/4 (3.5mm) crochet hook

➔ 14 x 8in. (35 x 20cm) piece of batting (for two hangers)

➔ 2 wooden coat hangers

## Abbreviations

**ch** chain; **dc** double crochet; **hdc** half double crochet; **rep** repeat; **sc** single crochet; **ss** slip stitch; **st(s)** stitch(es); **yo** yarn over hook

## Special abbreviations

**2ch picot** 2ch, ss into second ch from hook, pull tight

**3ch picot** 3ch, ss into third ch from hook, pull tight

**dcCl** (double crochet cluster) *yo, insert hook through ring, yo, pull yarn through 2 loops (2 loops on hook); rep from * twice more (4 loops on hook), yo, pull yarn through all 4 loops (1 double crochet cluster made)

## Size

**To fit hanger:** approx. 12½in. (31cm) long

## Finished size

**Length:** 12½in. (31cm)

## Cover (both hangers)

Using A or F, make 14ch.

**Row 1:** 3ch (counts as first dc), 1dc in fifth ch from hook, 1dc in each ch to end, turn.

**Row 2:** 3ch (counts as first dc), 1dc in each dc to last st, 1dc in top of previous 3-ch, turn.

**Row 3:** Rep Row 2 another 27 times or until work is long enough to cover coat hanger. Fasten off.

## Small watermelon chunks (make 9)

Using C, 4ch, 2dc in first ch.

Fasten off.

Join in D, 1ch, 1sc in top of first dc, 2sc in second dc, 1sc in top of fourth ch.

Fasten off.

Join in B, 1ch, 2sc in each of next 4 sts.

Fasten off.

Using E, hand sew 3 sts on each chunk.

## Watermelon large chunks (make 2)

Using C, 4ch, 1hdc, 2dc, 1hdc in first ch.

Fasten off.

Join in D, 1ch, 1sc in top of first st, 2sc into each of next 4 sts, ss into second of 4-ch from previous row. (9 sts)

Fasten off.

Join in B, skip 1 st, 2sc in each of next 8 sts. (16 sts)

Fasten off.

Using E, hand sew 3 sts on each chunk.

### Large leaf (make 2 or more)

Using B, make 12ch.

**Row 1**: 1sc in third ch from hook, 1hdc in next st, 1dc in each of next 6 sts, 1hdc in next st, sc into end ch.

**Row 2**: 2ch, working down other side of base chains, 1sc into first st, 1hdc in next st, 1dc in each of next 6 sts, 1hdc in next st, 1ch, ss into next ch.

Fasten off.

### Small leaf (make 18)

Using B, make 10ch,

**Row 1**: 1sc in third ch from hook, 1hdc in next st, 1dc in each of next 4 sts, 1hdc in next st, 1sc in end ch.

**Row 2**: 2ch, working down other side of base chains, 1sc in first st, 1hdc in next st, 1dc in next 4 sts, 1hdc in next st, 1ch, ss in next ch.

Fasten off.

### Hens (make 3)

Using H, make 4ch.

**Row 1**: 5dc into first ch, turn.

**Row 2**: 3ch, 2dc in each of next 2 sts, 1dc in each of next 2 sts, 2dc in next st, 1dc in last st, turn.

**Row 3**: 3ch, 1tr in first st, 1dc in next st, 1hdc in next st, ss in each of next 4 sts, 2ch, 3ch picot, 1tr in same st, 3ch picot, 1dc in next st, 3ch picot, 2ch, ss in last st.

Fasten off.

Rejoin yarn in top of hdc on hen's head.

2ch, 1dc in each of next 2 sts, 2ch, ss into same st.

Fasten off.

**Legs:**

Using I and with RS facing, join yarn to middle of bottom edge of hen's body.

*3ch, [2ch picot] twice, ss in first ch of 2-ch; rep from * once more, ss back in bottom edge.

Fasten off.

**Beak:**

Join J to bottom of 2ch, 2ch picot.

Fasten off.

**Under beak:**

Join K to top of 3ch, 3ch picot.

Fasten off.

**Comb:**

Join K to top of head, [3ch picot] twice, ss in top of head.

Fasten off.

### Chicks (make 6)

Using H, make 9ch.

Ss into sixth ch from hook, 1dcCl into first ch, 3ch ss into first ch.

Fasten off.

**Feet:**

Using I and with RS facing, join yarn to middle of bottom edge of chick's body.

*4ch, ss into second ch, ss into first ch; rep from * once, ss back in bottom edge.

Fasten off.

### Small flowers (make 2)

Make 4ch, join with ss to make a ring, 6sc in ring.

*Ss into first sc, 3ch, 1dc into same st, 3ch, ss into same st; rep from * five times. (6 petals)

Fasten off.

**Finishing**

Cover wooden part of coat hanger with a layer of batting to pad.

Place crocheted cover around batting and work sc to join along bottom edge.

Fasten off.

Sew in ends on all crochet pieces.

**Watermelon cover edging and hook embellishments**

Join B to one end of bottom of coat hanger cover, make 4ch.

Put hook through middle of top of small watermelon chunk, pull yarn through and make fifth ch, make 4ch. Measure 1¼in. (3cm) along bottom of hanger and join ch to cover with sc. Repeat to add remaining small chunks.

Fasten off.

**Loops:**

Using B, join yarn in work near base of hook. Make 30ch, ss back in work near hook, make 25ch, ss back in work near hook, make 27ch, ss back in work near hook.

Fasten off.

**Leaves:**

Place leaves at base of coat hanger hook and stitch in position. Stitch large watermelon chunks between leaves.

Sew in ends.

**Chicken cover edging and hook embellishments**

Using I, embroider eyes on hen and chicks. Join 1 hen, 3 chicks, 1 hen, 3 chicks, 1 hen together in order.

Join G to one end of bottom edge of coat hanger cover, ss through tail of hen, *make

12ch, ss through comb of same hen and back in base of coat hanger 2⅜in. (6cm) from end of hanger. Make 8ch, ss in bottom edge of coat hanger cover approx. 3½in. (9cm) from end, make 8ch, ss in next hen tail and back in bottom edge of coat hanger cover; rep from * twice more.

Fasten off.

**Leaves:**

Place leaves at base of coat hanger hook and stitch in position, then place flowers on top of leaves around base of the coat hanger hook and stitch in position.

Sew in ends.

# Happy Stars Crib Garland

This is a beautiful garland to hang in a baby's room. Drape it over the top of the crib for your baby to look at the beautiful colors and dangly flowers, or hang along the ceiling or wall.

## Materials

**50% baby alpaca/50% merino wool mix worsted (Aran) yarn, such as Rooster Almerino Aran**

➔ 1 x 1¾oz (50g) ball—approx. 103yds (94m)—of orange (MC), bright pink, pale gray, blue, pale green, and lilac

**50% baby alpaca/50% merino mix light worsted (DK) yarn, such as Rooster Almerino DK**

➔ 1 x 1¾oz (50g) ball—approx. 124yds (113m)—of bright orange

➔ G/6 (4.5mm) crochet hook and D/3 (3mm) crochet hook

## Abbreviations

**ch** chain; **dc** double crochet; **hdc** half double crochet; **MC** main color; **rep** repeat; **sc** single crochet; **sp** space; **ss** slip stitch; **st(s)** stitch(es)

## Finished size

**Length**: 56in. (142cm) long

## Stars (make 4 in each color)

Using G/6 (4.5mm) hook, 6ch, join circle with ss in first ch.

**Round 1**: 1ch [1sc in circle, 3ch] 12 times, ss in first sc.

**Round 2**: Ss in each of next 2 ch, 1ch, 1sc in 3-ch sp from previous round [3ch, 1sc in next 3-ch sp] 11 times. 1ch, 1hdc in top first sc.

**Round 3**: *6ch, 1sc in next 3-ch sp**, 3ch, 1sc in next 3-ch sp from previous round; rep from * 4 more times and from * to ** once more, 1ch, 1dc in hdc that closed previous round.

**Round 4**: *[5dc, 2ch, 5dc] in next 6-ch sp, 1sc in next 3-ch sp; rep from * 5 more times, ending last rep in dc that closed previous round, ss in next st.

Fasten off.

## Joining

Lay stars out in a row. Sew each star to the next one at the middle two points, using a yarn needle.

Using MC, make 50ch.

Do not fasten off.

With right side of garland facing and starting at the right-hand side, insert hook in middle space of top point of first star and make 1sc to join chain to star.

Make *15ch, 1sc in middle space of top point of next star; rep from * to last star, make 50ch for tie.

Fasten off.

## Flowers (make 2 in each color)

Using D/3 (3mm) hook, make 4ch, join with a ss to form a ring.

Make 5sc in ring, join with ss.

Ss in first st, *2ch, 1hdc, 2ch, ss in same st, ss in next st; rep from * 4 more times.

Fasten off.

## Finishing

Sew in ends.

# Baby Cloths

These are handy and pretty little cloths to take around in your baby bag—so lovely you'll put everyone else's fabric cloths to shame. I adapted these traditional square patterns from vintage patterns found in my mother's craft drawer that were due for a well-earned airing.

 Beginner

## Traditional square

### Materials

**100% cotton light worsted (DK) yarn, such as Rowan Handknit DK**

## Traditional square

Using A, make 4ch, join with ss to form a ring.

**Round 1**: 3ch (counts as first dc), 2dc in ring, 2ch, *3dc in ring, 2ch; rep from * twice; join with ss in first 3-ch.

Join in B.

**Round 2**: Ss in first 2-ch sp, 3ch [1dc, 2ch, 3dc] in same ch sp, 1ch; *[3dc, 2ch, 3dc] in next ch sp (corner), 1ch; rep from * twice, 1dc in next ch sp, join with ss. (4 corners).

Join in C.

**Round 3**: Ss in first 2-ch sp, 3ch [1dc, 2ch, 3dc] in same sp, 1ch, 3dc in next ch sp, 1ch, *[3dc, 2ch, 3dc] in next corner sp, 1ch, 3dc in next ch sp, 1ch; rep from * twice, 1dc in next ch sp; join with ss.

Alternate colors as set in each following row.

**Rounds 4–8**: Ss in first 2-ch sp, 3ch, [1dc, 2ch, 3dc] in same ch sp, 1ch, [3dc in next ch sp, 1ch] in each ch sp to corner, [3dc, 2ch, 3dc] in corner space; rep from * twice, 1dc in next ch sp; join with ss.

Fasten off.

### Finishing

➜ 1 x 1¾oz (50g) ball—approx. 93yds (85m)—each of pink (A), light blue (B), and mid-blue (C)

➜ G/6 (4.5mm) crochet hook

### Abbreviations

**ch** chain; **dc** double crochet; **rep** repeat; **sc** single crochet; **sp** space; **ss** slip stitch; **st(s)** stitch(es)

### Finished size

9in. (22.5cm) square

Improver

# Wave cloth

## Materials

**100% cotton light worsted (DK) yarn, such as Rowan Handknit DK**

→ 1 x 1¾oz (50g) ball—approx. 93yds (85m)—each of lilac (A), turquoise (B), pink (C), light blue (D), yellow (E), and mid-blue (F)

→ F/5 (4mm) crochet hook

## Abbreviations

**ch** chain; **dc** double crochet; **rep** repeat; **sp** space; **ss** slip stitch; **st(s)** stitch(es); **yo** yarn over hook

## Special abbreviation

**dc3tog** (double crochet 3 together decrease) *yo, insert hook in next st, yo, pull yarn through, yo, pull yarn through 2 loops on hook (2 loops on hook). Without finishing st, rep from * in each of next 2 sts (4 loops on hook), yo, pull yarn through all 4 loops on hook

## Finished size

9in. (22.5cm) square

# Wave cloth

Using A, make 33ch.

**Row 1**: 1dc in 2nd ch from hook, 1dc in next ch, *1dc in each of next 3 ch, dc3tog over next 3 sts, 1dc in each of next 3-ch, 3dc in next ch; rep from * ending last rep with 2dc in last ch. Fasten off.

**Row 2**: Join B into first st, 2ch, 1dc in first st, *1dc in each of next 3 sts, dc3tog over next 3 sts, 1dc in each of next 3 sts, 3dc in next st; rep from * ending last rep with 2dc in last ch. Fasten off.

**Row 3**: Join C into first st, 2ch, 1dc in first st, *1dc in each of next 3 sts, dc3tog over next 3 sts, 1dc in each of next 3 sts, 3dc in next st; rep from * ending last rep with 2dc in last ch.

Fasten off.

Work 15 rows of Row 2, changing color on each row.

Fasten off.

## Finishing

Sew in ends on wrong side. Block cloth.

# Floral Burst

Using A, make 6ch, join with ss in first ch to form a ring.

**Round 1**: 3ch (counts as first dc), 2dc in ring, 3ch, *3dc in ring, 3ch; rep from * 5 times more, join with ss in top of first 3-ch.

**Round 2**: With RS facing, join B, in any ch sp, 3ch, [2dc, 3ch, 3dc] in same ch sp, *[3dc, 3ch, 3dc] in next 3-ch sp; rep from * to end, join with ss in top of first 3-ch.

**Round 3**: Ss in each of next 2 sts, ss in next 3-ch sp, 3ch, 8dc in same ch sp, *[9dc in next 3-ch sp]; rep from * to end, join with ss in first ss.

Break yarn, do not fasten off.

**Round 4**: With RS facing, join C, 2ch (counts as first hdc), 1hdc in next st, 1sc in each of next 5 sts, 1hdc in each of next 2dc, 1tr in sp between next 3-dc groups on Round 2, *1hdc in each of next 2 sts on Round 3, 1sc in each of next 5 sts, 1hdc in each of next 2 sts, 1tr in sp between next 3-dc groups on Round 2; rep from * to last st, 1hdc, join with ss in first 2-ch.

**Round 5**: 3ch, 1dc in next hdc, 1dc in next sc, 2dc in each of next 3sc, *[1dc in each of next 7 sts, 2dc in each of next 3sc]; rep from * ending 1dc in each of last 4 sts, join with ss in top of first 3-ch.

**Round 6**: 3ch, 3dc in next st, *1dc in each of next 12 sts, 3dc in next st;; rep from * to end, join with ss in top of first 3-ch.

Break yarn, but do not fasten off.

**Round 7**: Join D, 1ch, skip next st, 5dc in next st, skip next st, * [1sc in next st, skip next st, 5dc in next st, skip next st]; rep from * to end, join with ss in first sc.

Fasten off.

### Finishing

Sew in ends. Block cloth.

Improver

## Floral burst

### Materials

**100% cotton light worsted (DK) yarn, such as Rowan Handknit DK**

→ 1 x 1¾oz (50g) ball—approx. 93yds (85m)—each of green (A), bright pink (B), purple (C), and off-white (D)

→ F/5 (4mm) crochet hook

### Abbreviations

**ch** chain; **dc** double crochet; **hdc** half double crochet; **rep** repeat; **RS** right side; **sc** single crochet; **sp** space; **ss** slip stitch; **st(s)** stitch(es)

### Finished size

9in. (22.5cm) diameter

Enthusiast

## Rose cloth
**Materials**

**100% cotton light worsted (DK) yarn, such as Rowan Handknit DK**

→ 1 x 1¾oz (50g) ball—approx. 93yds (85m)—of red (A), pink (B), lilac (C), and gray (D)

→ D/3 (3mm) crochet hook

**Abbreviations**

**ch** chain; **dc** double crochet; **hdc** half double crochet; **rep** repeat; **sc** single crochet; **sp** space; **ss** slip stitch; **st(s)** stitch(es)

**Finished size**

9in. (22.5cm) square

# Rose cloth

Using A, make 4ch join with ss in first ch to form a ring.

**Round 1**: *2ch, 4dc in ring, ss in ring; rep from * 3 times more. (4 petals)

**Round 2**: Ss in back of second dc, (keeping yarn at back of work) *4ch, ss in base of second dc of next petal; rep from * twice more, 4ch, ss in ss from Round 1.

**Round 3**: [1ss, 5dc, 1ss] in each loop (4 petals), join with ss in first ss.

Drop loop, break yarn, but do not fasten off.

**Round 4**: Join B, *6ch, 1ss in back of ss between petals; rep from * 3 times more.

**Round 5**: 3ch (counts as 1dc), [2dc, 2ch, 3dc] in first loop, *1ch, [3dc, 2ch, 3dc] in next loop; rep from * twice more, ss in top of first 3-ch.

Fasten off.

**Round 6**: Join C in any corner sp, 3ch (counts as 1dc), [2dc, 2ch, 3dc] in same sp, *[1ch, 3dc] in each 1-ch sp to next corner, [1ch, 3dc, 2ch, 3dc] in next corner; rep from * to end, ss to top of first 3-ch.

Fasten off.

**Round 7**: Join D in any corner sp, 3ch (counts as 1dc), [2dc, 2ch, 3dc] in same sp, *[1ch, 3dc] in each 1-ch sp to next corner, [1ch, 3dc, 2ch, 3dc] in next corner; rep from * to end, ss to top of first 3-ch.

Fasten off..

**Round 8**: Join B in any corner sp, 3ch (counts as 1dc), [2dc, 2ch, 3dc] in same sp, *[1ch, 3dc] in each 1-ch sp to next corner, [1ch, 3dc, 2ch, 3dc] in next corner; rep from * to end, ss to top of first 3-ch.

Fasten off.

**Round 9**: Join C in any corner sp, 3ch (counts as 1dc), [2dc, 2ch, 3dc] in same sp, *[1ch, 3dc] in each 1ch sp to next corner, [1ch, 3dc, 2ch, 3dc] in next corner; rep from * to end, ss to top of first 3-ch.

Fasten off.

**Round 10**: Join D in any corner sp, 3ch (counts as 1dc), [2dc, 2ch, 3dc] in same sp, *[1ch, 3dc] in each 1-ch sp to next corner, [1ch, 3dc, 2ch, 3dc] in next corner; rep from * to end, ss to top of first 3-ch.

Fasten off.

**Round 11**: Join B in any corner sp, 3ch (counts as 1dc), [2dc, 2ch, 3dc] in same sp, *[1ch, 3dc] in each 1-ch sp to next corner, [1ch, 3dc, 2ch, 3dc] in next corner; rep from * to end, ss to top of first 3ch.

Fasten off.

**Finishing**

Sew in ends. Block cloth.

# Billy the Bear

Billy is a happy bear made in rounds. He's very squidgy and easy to carry—don't over-stuff him, he should be lovely, soft, and cuddly; break the stuffing into small pieces before inserting.

## Materials

**50% baby alpaca/50% merino mix light worsted (DK) yarn, such as Rooster Almerino DK**

→ 1 x 1¾oz (50g) ball—approx. 124yds (112.5m)—each of pale blue, pale pink, blue-green, yellow, red, off-white, and green

→ E/4 (3.5mm) crochet hook

→ Pair safety eyes

→ Fiberfill stuffing

→ Scrap of black yarn for face details

## Abbreviations

**ch** chain; **rep** repeat; **RS** right side; **sc** single crochet; **sc2tog** (single crochet 2 together decrease) insert hook in next st, yo, pull yarn through (2 loops on hook). Without finishing st, insert hook in next st, yo, pull yarn through (3 loops on hook), yo, pull yarn through all 3 loops on hook; **st(s)** stitch(es); **ss** slip stitch; **WS** wrong side

## Finished size

**Length**: approx. 13½in. (34cm) tall

## Gauge

20 x 15 rows over a 4in. (10cm) square working in single crochet using a E/4 (3.5mm) hook.

## Head

Alternate colors every round, except for Rounds 1–2 and 25–26, which are the same.

Using first color, make 2ch.

**Round 1**: 6sc in second ch from hook. (6 sts)

Place st marker at beg of each round (loop on hook counts as one st).

**Round 2**: 2sc in each st. (12 sts)

Change color on next and every following round.

**Round 3**: *1sc in first st, 2sc in next st; rep from * to end. (18 sts)

**Rounds 4–5**: 1sc in each st.

**Round 6**: *1sc in each of next 2 sts, 2sc in next st; rep from * to end. (24 sts)

**Rounds 7–8**: 1sc in each st. (24 sts)

**Round 9**: 1sc in each of next 7 sts, 2sc in each of next 10 sts, 1sc in each of next 7 sts. (34 sts)

**Round 10**: *1sc in next st, 2sc in next st; rep from * once more, 1sc in each of next 25 sts, 2sc in next st, 1sc in each of next 2 sts, 2sc in next st, 1sc. (38 sts)

**Round 11**: 1sc in each of next 11 sts, 2sc in next st, *1sc in each of next 2 sts, 2sc in next st, rep from * 4 times more, 1sc in each of next 11 sts. (44 sts)

**Rounds 12–18**: 1sc in each st. (44 sts)

**Round 19**: 1sc in next st, sc2tog, 1sc in each of next 2 sts, sc2tog, 1sc in each of next 30 sts, sc2tog, 1sc in next 2 sts, sc2tog, 1sc. (40 sts)

**Round 20**: 1sc in each of next 11 sts, sc2tog, 1sc in next 2 sts, sc2tog, 1sc in each of next 6 sts, sc2tog, 1sc in each of next 2 sts, sc2tog, 1sc in each of next 11 sts. (36 sts)

**Round 21**: 1sc in each st. (36 sts)

**Round 22**: *1sc in each of next 4 sts, sc2tog; rep from * to end. (30 sts)

**Round 23**: *1sc in each of next 3 sts, sc2tog; rep * to end. (24 sts)

Insert eyes in 9th row from nose and stuff head.

**Round 24**: *1sc in each of next 2 sts, sc2tog; rep * to end. (18 sts)

**Round 25**: *1sc in next st, sc2tog; rep from * to end. (12 sts)

Do not change color.

**Round 26**: Sc2tog around. (6 sts)

Fasten off with a long tail approx. 6in. (15cm). Finish stuffing head then use yarn needle to thread tail through sts of last round to close gap neatly.

Sew in ends.

## Ears (make 4)

Do not count loop on hook as one st on this section—st marker is not necessary.

Using off-white only, make 2ch, 6sc in second ch from hook (do not join ring), turn. (6 sts)

**Row 1**: 1ch, 1sc in next st, 2sc in each of next 4 sts, 1sc in last st. (10 sts)

**Row 2**: 1ch, 2sc in first st, *1sc in next 2 sts, 2sc in next st; rep from * twice more. (14 sts)

Fasten off.

**Join ears to head:**

Place two ears with WS together, join yarn in one corner by pushing hook through both ears.

1ch, work 1sc around by pushing hook through both ears to join semicircle top of ears. Ss in bottom corner of semicircle to join.

Rep with other set of ears.

Fasten off. Sew ears onto head.

## Body

Alternate colors every round, except for Rounds 1 and 2 and 30 and 31, which are the same.

Using first color, make 2ch.

**Round 1**: 6sc in second ch from hook, join round and each subsequent round with ss. (6 sts)

**Round 2**: 2sc in each st. (12 sts)

Change color on next and every following round.

**Round 3**: *1sc in next st, 2sc in next st; rep from * to end. (18 sts)

**Round 4**: *1sc in each of next 2 sts, 2sc in next st; rep from * to end. (24 sts)

**Rounds 5–7**: 1sc in each st. (24 sts)

**Round 8**: 1sc in next st, 2sc in next st, *1sc in each of next 3 sts, 2sc in next st; rep from * to last 2 sts, 1sc in each st. (30 sts)

**Rounds 9–10**: 1sc in each st. (30 sts)

**Round 11**: *1sc in each of next 4 sts, 2sc in next st; rep from * to end. (36 sts)

**Rounds 12–13**: 1sc in each st (36 sts)

**Round 14**: *1sc in each of next 5 sts, 2sc in next st; rep from * to end. (42 sts)

**Rounds 15–17**: 1sc in each st. (42 sts)

**Round 18**: 1sc in each of next 8 sts, 2sc in next st, *1sc in each of next 4 sts, 2sc in next st; rep from * 4 more times, 1sc in each st to end. (48 sts)

**Rounds 19–22**: 1sc in each st. (48 sts)

**Round 23**: 1sc in each of next 3 sts, sc2tog, *1sc in each of next 6 sts, sc2tog; rep from * 4 times more, 1sc in each st to end. (42 sts)

**Round 24**: 1sc in each st. (42 sts)

**Round 25**: 1sc in each of next 4 sts, sc2tog, *1sc in each of next 9 sts, sc2tog; rep from * twice more, 1sc in each of next 3 sts. (38 sts)

**Round 26**: 1sc in each of next 3 sts, sc2tog, *1sc in each of next 8 sts, sc2tog; rep from * twice more, 1sc in each of next 3 sts. (34 sts)

**Round 27**: 1sc in each of next 3 sts, sc2tog, *1sc in each of next 7 sts, sc2tog; rep from * twice more, 1sc in each of next 2 sts. (30 sts)

**Round 28**: 1sc in each st. (30 sts)

**Round 29**: *1sc in each of next 3 sts, sc2tog; rep from * to end. (24 sts)

Stuff body.

**Round 30**: *1sc in each of next 2 sts, sc2tog; rep from * to end. (18 sts)

Do not change color.

**Round 31**: *1sc in each of next st, sc2tog; rep from * to end. (12 sts)

**Round 32**: Sc2tog around. (6 sts)

Fasten off with a long tail approx. 6in. (15cm). Finish stuffing body and use yarn needle to thread tail through sts of last round to close gap neatly.

## Legs (make two)

**Round 1**: 2ch, 6sc in second ch from hook.

**Round 2**: 2sc in each st. (12 sts)

**Round 3**: *2sc in first st, 1sc in next st; rep from * to end. (18 sts)

**Round 4**: *2sc in first st, 1sc in each of next 2 sts; rep from * to end. (24 sts)

**Round 5–6**: 1sc in each st. (24 sts)

**Round 7**: *Sc2tog, 1sc in next st; rep from * to end. (16 sts)

**Round 8**: 1sc in each st. (16 sts)

Rep Round 8 until work measures approx. 4½in. (12cm).

Fasten off.

**Arms (make two)**

Rep pattern as for legs.

Fasten off.

**Finishing**

Sew in ends.

Embroider nose and mouth detail. Pin pieces in place first to check positioning. Sew body to head with widest part at bottom. Stuff legs and arms and attach to body.

### EXPERT ADVICE

*Use safety eyes or embroider eyes—the bear may reach little hands or little mouths.*

*Slip stitch at the end of each round in last stitch.*

*To join colors keep the loop on the hook, place the hook in the next stitch, and then use the new color.*

# Suppliers

The yarns used in these projects should be available from your local yarn or craft store. If you can't find the correct yarn, try some of the websites listed here.

WEB SITES
**Debbie Bliss**
www.debbieblissonline.com

**Coats Craft Rowan Yarns**
www.coatscrafts.co.uk

**Purl Soho**
www.purlsoho.com

**Yarn Forward**
www.yarnforward.com

**Fyberspates**
www.fyberspates.co.uk

**Laughing Hens**
www.laughinghens.com

US STOCKISTS
**Bluefaced Leicester**
Wool2Dye4
6000-K Boonsboro Road
Coffee Crossing
Lynchburg
VA 24503
www.wool2dye4.com

**Knitting Fever**
Stockists of Debbie Bliss, Noro, and Sirdar yarns
www.knittingfever.com

**The Knitting Garden**
Stockists of Rowan yarns
www.theknittinggarden.com

**Lets Knit**
www.letsknit.com

**WEBS**
www.yarn.com

**Yarn Market**
www.yarnmarket.com

**Unicorn Books and Crafts**
www.unicornbooks.com

**A.C. Moore**
Stores nationwide
1-888-226-6673
www.acmoore.com

**Crafts, etc.**
Online store
1-800-888-0321
www.craftsetc.com

**Hobby Lobby**
Stores nationwide
www.hobbylobby.com

**Jo-Ann Fabric and Craft Store**
Stores nationwide
1-888-739-4120
www.joann.com

**Michaels**
Stores nationwide
1-800-642-4235
www.michaels.com

UK STOCKISTS
**Rooster Yarns**
Laughing Hens online
Wool, patterns, knitting & crochet supplies.
www.laughinghens.com
+44 (0)1829 740903

**Laughing Hens**
(wool, hooks, accessories)
The Croft Stables
Station Lane
Great Barrow
Cheshire CH3 7JN
+ 44 (0)1829 740903
www.laughinghens.com

**Fyberspates**
Unit 6 Oxleaze Farm Workshops
Broughton Poggs
Filkins
Lechlade
Glos GL7 3RB
07540 656660
www.fyberspates.co.uk

**Rowan Yarns**
Green Lane Mill
Holmfirth
West Yorkshire HD9 2DX
+44 (0)1484 681881
www.knitrowan.com

**John Lewis**
Stores nationwide
+44 (0)845 604 9049
www.johnlewis.com

TUITION
**Nicki Trench Workshops**
Crochet, knitting, and craft workshops for all levels
Email: nicki@nickitrench.com

# Index

# Acknowledgments

My own babies are all grown up now and I don't have grandchildren yet, but I have really indulged in designing such a cute crochet book.

Making this book has been a real team effort and I'm privileged to have worked with such an enthusiastic and talented group of people. I'm indebted to my expert crocheters who helped enormously to get the projects finished in time: Carolyn Meggison, Sue Lumsden, Duriye Foley, Emma Lightfoot, Laura Ramage, and Fran Wensel.

I've had enormous support from Andy Robinson and John Okell from Laughing Hens who supplied all the Rooster Yarns with such prompt and efficient service and who sent out to all the crocheters at a minute's notice.

Huge thanks also to Marie Clayton for her patience and expert editing and to Pat Cooper for stepping in and sorting out the pattern grading with prompt attention.

Thank you to all those at Cico Books for trusting me with yet another book project, especially to Cindy Richards, Pete Jorgensen, and Sally Powell for putting together such a pretty book with incredible efficiency.

And the biggest thank you goes out to my amazing mother Beryl, for her hawk's eye at checking the patterns and diligence at working out patterns and crocheting like crazy to meet the deadlines and for her unquestioning support.